She Called
MY NAME

DON AND JUDY BAILEY

PRESS

Map of Medjugorje by Blake F. Bailey
Cover design by Sara Grant.
Cover Photos Used with license permission.
All other photos by E. Don Bailey
Author photo by Scott Brouwer
www.JudyandDonBailey.com

www.xulonpress.com

DEDICATION

To our sons, Blake and Devon- Thank you for your love and patience with us as we worked together on the writing of this book and as the Lord continues to work on perfecting us as parents. You have enriched our journey though this life beyond measure. We hope that this book will bring assurance and hope of God's eternal love and care for each of you and that it will serve as a legacy to you and your future children's children. May it bless you and many generations to come.

May you be blessed by your Creator who saw all that he had made {including you} and called it very good!

Our Sons, Blake F. Bailey, Devon P. Bailey

Testimonials

Rev. Msgr. Michael A. Cherup, Diocese of
Pensacola-Tallahassee

"God plants seeds of faith – it is up to us to continually water
the seed. In the book She Called My Name, Judy and Don
Bailey, two Protestant's did just this by answering a call to go
on a trip to Medjugorje. The amazing blessings they received
from the trip allowed their faith to grow and blossom in their
lives as individuals and as a married couple. Be blessed as
you take the journey with them and let your seed of faith be
watered as well." Rev. Msgr. Michael A. Cherup

Bob Schuchts PHD, LMFT Therapist, Consultant, Theology
of the Body Healing and Training Center

"Amazing...miraculous...life-changing...awe-inspiring!
These are the words that come to mind when I think

about Don and Judy's experiences, which you will soon encounter for yourself. When I first heard Don and Judy's story, I believed them with my whole heart. Though it has been twenty-one years, they have not embellished the story in any way. I truly believe that the events you are about to read are true and accurate, and may very well leave an indelible impression on you, as they did on me."

Ron and Cathy Harrell, Grace to Glory International Ministries, Inc.

"God is always on a "Mission Trip" to meet his children right where they are but, he never leaves them there. He took Don and Judy from their "Protestant homeland" on a Catholic pilgrimage to encounter Him in a whole new way. Their journey to Medjugorje renews our faith that God is bigger than we thought. As missionaries we know that you never return the same."

Acknowledgements

First, a special thanks to Bob Schuchts. Bob was praying for us long before we ever knew. His continued prayers, support and teachings have been a substantial and positive spiritual blessing on our lives and his encouragements helped us throughout the writing of this book.

To Terri, we will always be grateful for your courage and obedience in delivering Judy the message you were given. We will forever have a special place in our hearts for the memories of the time we spent with you sharing this incredible journey.

To everyone that shared this pilgrimage to Medjugorje with us in August of 1990. Lois, Mary, Linda, Barbara, Terri, Charlie, Marian, Jamie, Holly, Mike, Page, John, Irene, Hal, and Fr. Mike. After twenty-one years we have scattered in many directions but you will forever be a part of this story and our family in Christ. And, to the memory of our travel companions Anita and Henry who have since departed this life and joined the saints in Heaven.

To Janet Gow, our coach, who consistently gave us encouragement and direction and always encouraged us to be our best self. Your unselfish dedication in always giving your best was the best example anyone could ever have.

To Scott Brouwer, our friend and photographer, for the early morning photographs to be used for this book and our website. Your works have always impressed us and your sense of humor makes it impossible not to smile.

To Sara Grant for your diligent and creative work on our book cover. Thanks for your willingness to work with us on some hectic deadlines and the grace you always exhibited with our constant "can you do just one more thing?"

To our friends who read our first drafts and gave us some incredible feedback which made us realize the book wasn't quite finished. Because of you we added chapters, explained things better and removed more "thats" and "hads" than we care to remember. Thank you Ron and Cathy Harrell, Lisa Miller, Fr. Eric Dudley, Lois Shovlain, Bob Schuchts, Rev. Michael A. Cherup and Anne Elizabeth Hall.

To our editors, many thanks for leading us through this process. Thanks to Janet Gow, Ann Elizabeth Hall and a special thanks to Sean Whiteford for the final edit.

To God our Father, we forever will give you thanks for answering our prayers and orchestrating the events of this story and for making our family complete with the gift of our son Devon. This is the story You wrote for all of our lives and we pray that generations in our family and all readers will be blessed.

To The Virgin Mary, we give thanks for her continued prayers for our world and for her tireless pleas to draw us closer to her Son. We give thanks that through her call she taught us that she is the gentle Mother to all Christians even those outside the Roman Catholic Church.

To Jesus, who paid the greatest price for us all, our gratitude for a love that is so large we will never be able to comprehend it this side of Heaven.

To God be the Glory! Amazing things He has done!

Don and Judy Bailey

Forward by Bob Schuchts

After twenty-one years, I can't believe it is finally here! That is how long I have been waiting to hold this book in my hands. And though I had remembered almost every detail of every event described in this book, I still didn't want to put it down. (I had to stop twice, but I couldn't wait to get back to it). I have only read a few books in my fifty-six years of life where I couldn't wait to turn the page. This is one of those books. When you read it, you will see why.

Amazing...miraculous...life-changing...awe-inspiring! These are the words that come to mind when I think about Don and Judy's experiences, which you will soon encounter for yourself. When I first heard Don and Judy's story, I believed them with my whole heart. Though it has been twenty-one years, they have not embellished the story in any way. I truly believe that the events you are about to read are true and accurate, and may very well leave an indelible impression on you, as they did on me.

Allow me to give you a little background. My name is Bob Schuchts. I am the marriage and family therapist that Judy and Don refer to in their story. I have witnessed many miracles and heard of many supernatural encounters from the people I have counseled over the years, but Don and Judy's story is probably the most incredible of anything I have heard or witnessed. I have longed to see them share it with the rest of the world.

About twenty-nine years ago, I met Don Bailey who was going through a painful divorce at the time. I saw in Don a man with a heart of gold; but that heart was deeply buried behind walls of cynicism, despair, and anger. He was a difficult person to help, because he didn't listen well or trust very much. And yet, somehow, through all the difficulties of his divorce, he came to trust me. Enough so, that when he and Judy needed a marriage counselor years later, he turned to me.

When I finally met Judy, I could see she was a good complement to Don. She was upbeat and cheerful, though I could see that she, too, was troubled. Both she and Don were struggling a lot. They were dealing individually with losses and hurt which they were unable to overcome. These past and recent hurts made it especially difficult for each of them to trust and be open to the other – though they seemed to genuinely desire to do so. What made it more difficult, from my vantage point, was they had no apparent relationship with God. (Though later, I would find out differently).

A few years before I met with Judy and Don, I had a life-changing spiritual experience of my own. I had always believed in God, but through this experience in 1988, I came to know His personal love for me. This is not a book about me, so I will spare the details, but this encounter with the Holy Spirit deeply impacted me and my own family, and the way I approached my work. Once you have a life-changing encounter like that, you want everyone to experience the same kind of love and joy.

As a therapist, I didn't want to impose my faith on anyone – though I desired it for each individual and couple I counseled. Furthermore, I believe that God is the answer to every relationship issue. Only love heals, and relationships are built on love and trust. Without a genuine relationship with God, it is impossible to have an authentic relationship with anyone else. All the theories and techniques I learned in my graduate training were useless apart from love. So I desired this for Don and Judy, just as I do for every individual and couple I counsel. But neither Don nor Judy ever mentioned God during our early counseling sessions. So out of respect for them, and obedience to the Holy Spirit,

I waited for the appropriate time to discuss any issues of faith. I waited for them to introduce the topic. In the meantime, I silently prayed in their presence and interceded for them at home in my personal prayer time. I didn't see an opening, until the day that Judy mentions in her account of the events in this book.

Here is how I remember it: Judy showed up for our appointment on time, we waited for Don, but for some reason he never came. It turned out that he had forgotten about the appointment. It was one of the rare times that I met with Judy alone. Looking back it was a beautifully orchestrated providence. Without Don present, Judy opened up like never before. She seemed to pour her heart out more freely that afternoon.

I sat there amazed as she shared her pain, and with it her deep hunger for God. I later learned that she had a personal relationship with Jesus as a child and teenager, but had suppressed it in her relationship with Don. In many ways she was searching for God, but she had begun to have serious doubts about whether God even existed. The combination of unanswered prayers during some painful experiences had left her feeling separated from Him. What I heard that afternoon in 1990 was a woman who desperately wanted to know if God was there. She was longing for someone to discuss this with – she needed a spiritual comrade. She had been starving for a nourishing spiritual conversation.

This was the answer to my prayers, because I had a confidence that this was the missing piece in Judy's life. I mostly listened as she shared her pain and her longing, and at the end I asked her if she would be open to praying together. I sensed in her a desire for that, but since Judy was still shaken in her faith, I offered to pray *for* her. As I recall I offered this very simple and straightforward prayer on her behalf: "Father, I ask you to show Judy that you are real, and to provide her with a spiritual friend with whom she can share her faith. Thank you. I ask this in Jesus' name. Amen."

I was confident that God would answer this prayer because he had done so for me just a few years earlier. But little did either of us realize how quickly and profoundly this simple prayer would be answered. I was absolutely amazed the next time I saw Judy. Once again she came alone. For whatever human reason Don didn't come again, it was soon apparent that God had His own reasons. From the moment I saw Judy's face, I could see that everything about her was different. Her countenance had completely changed. I could see the joy and peace on her face that had been so absent since I met her. She spent the next 60 minutes sharing the amazing events that jump-started the story which you are about to read. This is Judy and Don's story to tell – so I invite you to hear it first hand from them.

Bob Schuchts
PHD, LMFT Therapist, Consultant

INTRODUCTION
By Judy Bailey

As we drove away from Medjugorje I sat quietly within my own thoughts looking out the window as we passed by St. James Church for the last time. I was filled with a strange combination of emotions. I could not expect anyone to understand what was going on inside me or comprehend how in just one week's time my entire world could so drastically change. There was no one, save those who had been on this trip with me, who could begin to understand. On the one hand, I was heading back to our new home in Florida and to the community I was so immersed in. On the other, it felt like I was leaving a loving oasis and people that I had uniquely bonded with over the course of just a few days. The intimacy of the relationships and experiences we had shared with strangers from all over the world had profoundly touched me and changed me in ways that some of my closest and most treasured friendships and relations back home never would. At the time I'm not sure if I realized it or not, but part of my heart would never leave this place where God had manifested his love for all of us in so many beautiful ways. Looking back at the village I had no idea how often I would find myself, in the future, pondering what had happened here and asking myself why God gave us these gifts- gifts we never could have thought possible or imagined to ask for. This week had filled me with such joy but there was also a pensive sense of wonderment. What had we done to receive such divine blessings? I knew the truth- we had done nothing to deserve this! While I was exhilarated and happy, I also felt a silent humbleness deep within me as I realized that what we had been given was an unmerited gift of God's favor and love. I was grateful but it was hard to comprehend.

There was still one last thing we were going to do together before we completely left the area. We were to stop at a tiny chapel, called Silver Chapel, which was tucked away in a rural area on the drive away from Medjugorje. In this quaint chapel we would have a final and private celebration of the Mass with only those we had traveled here with. I say traveled loosely because by now our journey had turned out to be a true pilgrimage in every sense of the word. The intimacy of the Mass carried both the joy and sadness we were all feeling as we realized we would never all be together again. The Mass was going to be special for another reason too. One of our new friends was going to be baptized and receive her first communion here. It was a fitting way to end the week that had been filled with so much grace.

When Mass was over, everyone took some final photographs of each other as well as a group picture with each other's cameras. Before we got back on the bus I decided to pull Terri and Page off to the side, away from the others, to talk. Terri and Page were two of my employees in the life we had back home. I realized that within a few days the three of us would be back into that life at work and into our normal routines. I also knew that my relationship with them would never be the same- not after this week. The things we had shared during our week in Medjugorje would forever transcend our work relationship. Standing in our small circle outside the chapel, I talked to them briefly about what it might be like when we returned and were faced with an office full of inquisitive people. I knew people at our office would be interested to hear about the journey we had taken halfway around the world together. We talked about how everyone would be pulling us aside and wanting to ask questions about our trip. We wanted to share with anyone who was interested, but we didn't want to create a circus or huge distractions with different people getting only bits and pieces of our story here and there. This was far too important to allow that to happen. We all agreed that it would be better to wait and share with everyone who had an interest at the same time. Page volunteered her house as the gathering place to meet once we returned home. When we finished talking, we held hands in our small circle and prayed for our safe travel and all the people who would be waiting for us back home.

Shortly after returning to work we made the announcement to the staff that we were going to be sharing some incredible things about our journey to Medjugorje and invited anyone interested to come. We settled on a date the following week. As far as we were concerned, this gathering would be our first and perhaps only time of sharing like this. But, it seems, God had other plans.

During our first week back we had been invited to join a prayer group that met on Wednesday nights at Good Shepherd Catholic Church in Tallahassee. As we arrived the evening Mass was just ending and we waited outside until the church had emptied. Within a few minutes we found ourselves inside a small chapel with others praying a beautiful prayer we had never heard before going on our trip. When the prayers were over we gathered outside the chapel and engaged in several casual conversations with those standing around. At one point, someone introduced us as part of a group who had just returned from Medjugorje. It was further explained to a few that my husband, Don, and

I were Protestants and that he had received some incredible experiences while there. The word spread quickly through the group of about thirty to forty people who were still standing outside. One person asked Don if he would share his experiences with them, and within a few minutes several people were asking him if he would go back inside the chapel and tell them everything. Suddenly, we found ourselves back inside the chapel and Don, the Protestant, was standing before this Catholic church group sharing everything that had happened to him.

As Don shared his moving story I could hardly believe this was the same man that had fought so vigorously about going to Medjugorje with me. After all of that, here he was, humbly standing in front of a group speaking boldly about his miraculous experience. When Don finished sharing, many people in the group came forward to talk with him. The last person to speak to him said she wanted to give him a hug for sharing his story. When Don hugged her she collapsed into his arms and began crying deep-seated tears. The following day we learned through a friend that as Don had put his arms around her she had a vision of Jesus in her spirit and felt as though she was falling into and being held in His arms.

After this the days flew by until it was time for the office gathering we had planned at Page's house. We realized that it was one thing to share our story with a group of believers, but this was going to be different- for sure! The radio business I worked in had always brought together a unique and diverse group of people- the fast-paced sales types, and the less than conventional and often entertaining on-air staff. Together this created a highly energized and interesting group and made for a fun, but often irreverent, office environment. I had more often shared drinks after work with these people and we had never discussed any issues of faith. I had no idea how my work friends and associates would react or how it might change my relationship with them afterward. Nevertheless, I was ready and a full house showed up that evening. I had known most of those attending for a long time and, as far as I could tell, most had no obvious spiritual or consistent religious life at the time.

Those of us who would be sharing decided to meet early to pray before everyone was to arrive. We were all somewhat apprehensive. We weren't sure how our close associates from work were going to receive some of the things we were prepared to tell them. I wondered what they would think when we shared many of the miracles we had witnessed. I wondered if some might not believe us. It was a professional risk, but even with the apprehensions I didn't seem to have any real concerns about telling them our story. In fact, we all seemed to share a boldness that enabled us to overcome any fear we might have. There seemed to be a grace and a covering that we were under and we realized that this too was going to be part of our journey.

As we began to tell our individual stories, one by one, the room was mostly silent with the exception of a few questions here and there. It was hard to read their reactions, but they seemed to be listening to everyone intently. What we thought would be a couple of hours of sharing had actually gone on very late into the evening. At one point, while Don was sharing his story, a couple with children looked at their watch, shocked, realizing the time and politely excused themselves, saying very little. In a few moments someone else left, excusing themselves, saying that they had to get up very early the next morning. As we all realized the lateness of the hour Don rapped up his portion of the talk and everyone began to gather their things and one by one they left. Some thanked us for sharing and some simply said good night. When everyone left (except those of us who had shared) we looked at each other and nervously laughed. It had been difficult for us to gauge what might have been on their minds as they left. Regardless, we were undaunted and we all felt at peace.

It was over the next few weeks that we began to realize the impact our sharing had had on many of those in attendance. The next day at work, a co-worker who had no obvious faith came to talk to me. She told me that she had never been moved by anything the way she had been moved the night before during our sharing. She had been to church a few times in her life, but nothing had ever reached into her heart or caused her to feel what she had felt after we shared our experiences. She and her boyfriend were one of the ones that had left so abruptly. She shared with me that they had moved their car just a few blocks away and had stopped to talk about what they were both feeling. She went on to say that they remained there, in their car, talking up into the wee hours of the morning. Their conversation centered on the things they had felt and witnessed during the time of sharing. Her boyfriend had been eager to leave because he needed to talk to her about something he had witnessed while Don was talking about his vision with Jesus. He himself had seen the appearance of Jesus with the wounds in his feet and hands standing in front of Don. He had been moved beyond words and was speechless. She also shared that she had seen what looked like a warm glow about Don at the same time. Another fellow employee shared with me that she was Catholic and had fallen away from her church. She told me how moved she had been and that she felt our sharing must have been much like the early days of the church. The early church had also been known to meet in individual homes to share their personal experiences with Jesus. She returned to her faith after this. Another luke-warm Christian found himself called to go deeper into his faith and later invited us to speak at his church's singles group about our experiences. He has since become a strong leader in his church. We continued to hear stories like this after we had shared our experiences with others.

Over the next few years we found ourselves being invited to share our story at churches and small groups or individual homes. We quickly realized that we were just the messengers and that God, through the Holy Spirit, was working things out in the lives of those we were asked to speak to. We felt that God had used us, through the gifts we received, to plant seeds in the hearts of those who were uncertain of His existence. Many people have shared with us that their small seed of faith had been lying dormant for years until our story came along and watered it with a fresh and timely message. A message concerning God's love for his people on earth and how the Virgin Mary is calling us to turn back to God and directing us to her Son.

It had been a prayer, sent from my own doubting heart, which seemed to have moved the heart of God. A prayer that needed to know if Jesus was truly who He said He was. As a Protestant, how could I imagine that He would use his Mother, the Virgin Mary, to deliver a personal invitation that would lead my husband and me half way around the world to discover the truth? My prayer was answered in the most remarkable way but God, in His mercy, did not choose to stop there. He also wanted to meet my husband and heal the wounded places of his heart. Through a miraculous vision, He exposed the lies that had been gripping his heart too. We were both amazed to look back and see the cookie trails that God had given each of us. He had beautifully orchestrated the people and miraculous events in this story to lead us individually to Him. Little did we understand at the time that He was weaving our two stories and our lives together in a way we never could have done without Him.

I now invite you to experience this journey with us; just as it happened twenty-one years ago. Through these pages you will experience the unexpected miracle that drew my husband and me (two backslidden Protestants) to the tiny village of Medjugorje in the first place. You will also read of some extraordinary miracles which we witnessed with our own eyes and which made the Bible come alive for us. The greatest miracle, however, was (and continues to be) the transformation of our hearts and the gift we received once we returned home.

This story was given to us but has now been written for you and it is our hope that it speaks to your heart too. We hope that through these pages you will begin to feel a new or greater awakening of your faith. We trust you will be refreshed and blessed as you go with us and share in this amazing journey that nourished and restored our souls in the summer of 1990.

TABLE OF CONTENT

Dedication v

Acknowledgements ix

Forward by Bob Schuchts.....................................xiii

Introduction to She Called My Name xix

Chapter 1   The Prayer That Started It All 33

Chapter 2   Seek and Ye Shall Find...............................41

Chapter 3   Three Hours That Changed My Life.........51

Chapter 4   The Conversation..59

Chapter 5   Conflicts, Confusion and Uncertainties ...67

Chapter 6   Our First Gathering 83

Chapter 7   The Journey Begins 89

Chapter 8   Medjugorje Arrival.....................................99

Chapter 9   A Mountain To Climb 127

Chapter 10   Hope Dashed 159

Chapter 11   The Secret..173

Chapter 12   Father Jozo...189

Chapter 13   Blinded By the Light 205

Chapter 14   The Sharing...221

Chapter 15   The Angels 235

Chapter 16   The Feast, Adoration and More 249

Chapter 17   Saying Good-Bye 267

Chapter 18   The Journey That Never Ends..................281

Chapter 19   Heart Reflections..297

Epilogue by Bob Schuchts.......................................309

Chapter 1

The Prayer That Started It All

JUDY

*A*pril 17, 1990 is a date I will always remember because I made a profound note in my journal. The note was the result of frustration, disappointment and confusion as well as what I would later come to call my crisis of faith. You see, I was questioning everything I had been taught to believe. I had been raised by Christian parents, taken to Sunday School and church every Sunday. My father was a deacon and my mother was the organist for all the Southern Baptist Churches in which we had been members. I had gone to church camps, helped in poor neighborhoods, attended Vacation Bible Schools, organized coffee houses for our youth group and sang in the youth choir. You name it, if something was going on, I was involved. I was even baptized TWICE. The first time, I was nine years old and had followed my friend

Elaine Bridges down to the front of the church during an alter call. As usual, in the Baptist tradition, we were baptized very soon after this. Then five years later, soon after turning fourteen, I felt my own personal call and realized that I had been following Elaine, and not really Jesus, the first time. It was very difficult for me to tell my parents and my pastor that I strongly believed I needed to do this. I had never heard of anyone asking to be baptized a second time before in my life but my heart was convinced this was the right thing to do. In the end, both my parents and pastor proved to be very supportive and so I was baptized a second time.

By most standards I was a good kid, full of fun mischievousness, just like my dad and my maternal granddad, but I also cared deeply about others. I had a heart for wanting to do the right things and I thought about God, a lot. Even still, now at the age of thirty-five I had begun to doubt it all. By this time the idea of living life according to "God's" ways had been pushed aside by the prevailing beliefs of many in my generation that- "if it feels good do it!" I had been exposed to a variety of spiritual ideas and my intellect was causing me to begin questioning whether any of this "Jesus stuff" was really true. By this time, I had completed college, been married and divorced and I was twelve years into a promising career in the radio business. Don and I had been married for eight months and I had just suffered another miscarriage.

Actually, it was an earlier miscarriage that convinced us that it was time to get married and start a family, which I wanted desperately. Don and I had been together almost seven years and were discussing marriage when we found out I was pregnant. The fact we were not married did not interfere with the joy and excitement I felt. I was thirty-four and, since neither of my parents were still living, it was a little easier for me to not worry about what anyone else thought. After all, this was almost the ninety's and I was a grown woman. Don's parents, however, were both still alive. I clearly remember the day we drove to their house to tell them the great news. Although I had some concern regarding how they would respond to the news, nothing was going to take away from the joy I was feeling. I was ecstatic and their approval or disapproval was not going to change that.

Don and I had decided to get away for the week-end at the beach to talk about how we were going to handle this unexpected surprise. On the drive home that Sunday afternoon, we drove over the Chattahoochee River Bridge and there was a huge rainbow arching over the bridge from one side of the river bed to the other. I felt like we were driving under and through it as we passed over the bridge. To me, it was a beautiful sign that all was well. Once we got to Don's parent's house, we went in and visited for a while. Finally, Don told them we had some news we wanted to share and invited them to come sit down in the living room. Don and I stood up together in the middle of the room as Don told them we were getting married and that I was pregnant. Don's dad was great with the news, but Edith, his mom, fell apart. She didn't know what to do. She didn't know what her friends would think because, "No one in her family had ever done 'THAT' before." I still remember Ernest scolding her and saying, "Good God Edith, shut up!" That was Don's Dad. He was not a man of many words, especially when he had a point to make. In a few minutes, she pulled herself together and we finally left thinking, "Well, that went well - NOT!" But nothing could prevent me from feeling so happy and excited about the new life that was growing in me.

Within a few weeks of this announcement, I began to have problems. My HCG hormone levels were not growing like they should in a healthy pregnancy. I could tell the doctor was worried, and soon so was I. With every blood test my excitement was turning to fear. One day, the HCG levels would spike up slightly and I would gain hope. Then it happened. I had been so apprehensive that day at work. I had a terrible uneasiness that something wasn't right. On the way home it was as if every cell in my body was vibrating and preparing itself for what was about to happen. Early that evening, at home, I miscarried and I was left heartbroken.

36

Don is not a typically sympathetic person, but during this time he had been so caring and tried his best to be understanding. His mother also came over to visit and to be supportive. She seemed genuinely upset and was blaming herself for not being supportive in the beginning. As bad as all this was, it provided us with a time to bond. The experience accomplished something else for Don and me. It made us both realize we were now ready to be married and start a family. We soon began making plans for our wedding in August of 1989. The wedding was simple and beautiful; it was on a Saturday morning outside at Oven Park in Tallahassee, Florida. After the wedding, we enjoyed a wonderful honeymoon in Bermuda and came back ready to start our married life, return to work and hopefully start working on our family.

Within a few months, I was happy, excited and pregnant again. But again, I had a miscarriage and within an eight month period I became pregnant three times. The first two had ended in miscarriages, so with the third we were doing everything to keep the pregnancy viable with hormone replacement therapy. Sadly, this pregnancy was ectopic and the doctor tried her best to assure me that the baby could not survive. I waited until the very last minute before I would agree to let the doctors perform a procedure that would remove the fetus, all the time hoping and praying they were wrong. Delaying this procedure resulted in me ending up in the Emergency

Room one evening with severe pain on my right side. When my doctor arrived, she told me the fetus was lodged in my fallopian tube and that I needed surgery immediately. After this, It began to look like I might never have a child, and that was a pain I was not prepared to face. I was devastated, depressed and so afraid. For me, those emotions almost always turn to anger, and this time was no exception. The anger was as fierce as the pain.

It was during this time I began to question everything about God and wondered if any of this "Jesus stuff" was really true. I felt like I had always been seeking Him, just like my Bible said to do, and yet it seemed to me that I was doing all the work. Where was He in all of this? I had prayed to Him earnestly each time I was pregnant but I still lost the babies. I didn't know why. Maybe He wasn't listening to me anymore. Maybe He wasn't even there. Even if He was there, I found myself having a hard time believing He cared about what was going on with me. I thought about how belief was much easier for those people who lived 2,000 years ago. They could talk to Jesus and ask Him direct questions. They could see Him perform miracles and look onto His face. They ran to His tomb and saw that He was gone. They saw Him resurrected and put their hands in His wounds. Here I was, 2,000 years later, and I was supposed to believe all this on blind faith - and I couldn't. If He was real, He would care about me. If He cared about me, He would not have let this happen. If He was real, where was He now when I needed Him to help me stay pregnant and to help me understand all of this? I wanted to sense His presence, but I didn't.

I was really growing weary of trying to understand the mystery of God and it seemed the searching was getting me nowhere. That's when I resolved that there were no attainable answers. I felt it would be a lot easier for me if I would just give it up and quit thinking about it. That's when I made up my mind and I wrote in my journal... "God, if you want me to believe in You, You are going to have to come down here and show me You want me. Show me that You're there. Show me that You care. I'm trying to believe but it's hard. I don't see You. I don't feel You. All I have is confusion and doubt and I'm tired of trying. I'm putting my Bible down and getting on with my life," -dated April 17, 1990.

That was it. I was done. The searching was not getting me anywhere. I was sad, disappointed and God wasn't there. At least, that's how it seemed to me. In a few days, I was back at work trying to put all of this out of my mind. I did, however, occasionally throw up a little prayer just in case someone actually happened to be listening. Perhaps this is what the Bible is referring to in the story of the mustard seed. I still had a very small seed of faith but it was getting smaller every day and I just wasn't sure how strong I believed anymore.

When he said to them, "Why are you troubled? And why do questions arise in your hearts?

Luke 24:38

The New American Bible

Chapter 2

Seek and Ye Shall Find

JUDY

A *month later, I was back in full throttle at work. The frustration and confusion I had been feeling was pushed to the back of my mind as I turned my energies back towards work. Part of this was deliberate, I know, because I had consciously made up my mind to quit worrying about God. It was during this time that the radio station's owners flew in to make a big announcement to our staff. They were selling the radio stations. Of course, this announcement made everyone predictably nervous, including our management team. It was not a secret that when new owners took over they often brought in their own managers. Still, as a manager, it was my responsibility to keep everyone positive and focused on the job at hand. This course of action, I hoped, would minimize any of the transitional concerns of my staff.*

The best thing we could do was to have everything in good shape and working order so, once our new owners arrived, they would recognize the great job we were doing.

It was during this tenuous time that Terri, an employee of mine, came into my office to request time off for a vacation. Our conversation became a little strained when I asked her if she was going somewhere fun. Her reply was a bit strange, and I could tell she was somewhat hesitant to share her plans with me. She answered by saying she was going somewhere in Yugoslavia with her mother. Of course, I was surprised, who wouldn't be? I naturally wondered why anyone would choose to vacation in Yugoslavia, and so I asked her why they were going there. Her reply was rather reluctant, but she stated that her mother was going with a friend who had gone just a few months earlier. She stated there had been healings at this place where, supposedly, there were six children who were reporting visitations from the Virgin Mary. Terri's mother now wanted to go back with this friend and Terri explained that her father had asked her to go along with them. It seemed she wanted me to understand that she was going more out of obligation than anything else. As we walked down the hall towards the coffee machine, I recall making a casual comment, something to the effect of "Well, you never know." Terri replied, "Yeah, maybe." By her tone, I surmised she was not convinced herself. The conversation ended here and within a couple of weeks Terri left for her trip. I never thought much more about our conversation after that.

During the next few weeks, I did, however, find myself thinking about Jesus again. He just wouldn't go away, no matter how much I tried to push Him out of my mind. I really wanted to talk to someone besides this invisible and quiet God that never seemed to answer my questions. I thought maybe I needed a spiritual advisor but had no idea where you would find one of those. I wanted someone I could trust who had a real faith - not necessarily a person with all the answers, just someone who truly walked the walk and who was "authentic." I tossed up one of those quick, almost unconscious prayers that are more of a thought than anything else. "Please send me someone to talk to".

There was one thing I knew for sure- I did not want to go to a minister or a priest. Although I had some very good memories of my time growing up and going to church, I had one memory I had just as soon forget. It was an experience I had in my pastor's office after school one afternoon when I was in the 11th grade. I really wasn't looking for any advice at the time, never-the-less, my Pastor and Youth Director both felt I needed some. I had been dating a boy who did not go to church, and let's say he was a lot of fun but a little on the wild side. My youth director and the Pastor decided this relationship was not going anywhere good and they felt they needed to intervene. They sent a note over to my high school asking me to please come by the church office after school. Not understanding why, I went and, once in the office, I felt completely overpowered by these two adults that I held in such high esteem. It was their opinion that this boy was going to have a bad influence on me and they presented two basic choices. I needed to start bringing him to church with me or I needed to break up with him. I can't remember everything they said to me, but I never remember them asking me how I felt. I don't remember them asking me anything. I do remember they did all the talking and they seemed to have all the answers. I left feeling quite sad and very upset because I cared about these two adults and I wanted them to think well of me. Looking back on this as an adult, I feel sure that my worried mother may have put them up to it. My dad had just passed away a year earlier, when I was sixteen, and I was turning into a strong-willed teenager who wanted to spread my wings and fly. I knew the odds of me getting my boyfriend to take church seriously were pretty slim; on the other hand, I couldn't think of one good reason why I should break up with him. To this day, I still think this incident is the reason I developed a serious case of Colitis and ended up in the hospital for a week. NO...I did not want this kind of an encounter. I was searching for someone who might have a spiritual connection to "the One" I was uncertain about. I was not interested in any kind of judgment or any pat answers for the solution to my deepest needs. There was no one I felt comfortable talking to or who I felt could help me find the answers I needed. So once again, I decided to just forget about it and throw myself into work.

Prior to getting married, Don and I had started going to see a counselor by the name of Bob Schuchts. Bob had been the marriage counselor that Don and his previous wife had also counseled with. Even though their marriage ended in divorce, Don trusted Bob and felt very comfortable with him. So, when we began to run into some of our own issues and I suggested we see a counselor, Don suggested we meet with Bob. Bob was great and right away I could see why Don liked him so much.

It was about a week before Terri had departed for her trip to Yugoslavia that I found myself sitting alone in Bob's office waiting on Don to arrive. Typically, Don would arrive before me so, after a few minutes, it became apparent that he had forgotten about our appointment. Bob suggested that we could proceed without Don. He asked me if there was anything on my mind that I wanted to talk about. I still had the lingering feelings of being abandoned by God during the miscarriages, but I wasn't sure I was at ease talking about it with Bob. With the exception of this and the nagging questions about the authenticity of Jesus, I couldn't think of any-

thing else I specifically needed to talk about. I had no idea what Bob's religious beliefs were. We had never talked about religion or faith; as far as I knew, Bob could have been an atheist. But there I was, feeling kind of stuck for something to talk about, so I reluctantly began by telling him I had some "spiritual things" going on. I also told him that I wasn't sure if he was the person I should be talking to about "these kind of things." Bob asked me what I meant by that. I explained that I didn't know what his faith was, or even if he had one. I'll never forget the big smile that appeared on his face as he said, "Well, why don't you just ask me then?" So I did. From there, Bob went on to tell me that Christ was the center of his life, as well as his counseling practice. He also told me that he prayed for each and every one of his clients. At that moment, I suddenly realized that, as his clients, unknown to me, he had been praying for us. He explained to me that he did not openly discuss his faith with his clients unless they brought it up first but that everything he did was centered on Christ.

"Wow," I thought. Here was Bob all this time and I had no idea. Now that I did, I began to share with him the things I had been through. This included my confusing questions and my doubts about God and specifically Jesus. Bob listened more than anything else that day, but before I left he asked me if I'd like to pray. I nodded my head yes although outside *of church or before a meal I had never prayed with anyone. Sensing my discomfort, he politely asked me if I'd like for him to lead us in prayer. I remember he prayed, "Father, show Judy that you are real and send her a friend with whom she can share her faith." I left our meeting that day feeling I had already found at least one "authentic" person able to help me with my searching. When I got home, I wrote Bob a thank you note and told him I had been praying for someone to talk to, a spiritual advisor or counselor. I couldn't imagine this would turn out to be someone I already knew. I had a tremendous amount of respect for Bob and, although I had not known he was a man of deep faith, it was obvious to me he possessed a quiet inner strength. I was extremely happy and grateful that I now had someone I could talk to about these spiritual things stirring in me.*

It was just a few days after this meeting with Bob, and during the week Terri was away in Yugoslavia, that I had a most unusual, vivid dream. In this dream, I saw a massive number of people making their way up a mountain on a treacherous stony path lined with large thorn bushes along the way. I never saw these people's faces. All I saw were their feet as they were walking up this path, but I knew they represented people from all over the world; men and women, all age groups and all races. The shoes were flip flops, old men's shoes, women's sandals, tennis shoes, boots, and every kind of shoe imaginable, even people who were walking with bare feet. The dream made quite an impression upon me because it had been so clear and detailed. It had no significant meaning to me at the time, so I forgot about it as we do with so many of our dreams.

Soon, the week had gone by and Terri was back from her trip. It was a typical Monday morning with sales meetings and everyone rushing to get things going with their week. It was not until the middle of the afternoon when I saw Terri passing by my office door. I called after her to ask if she had enjoyed her vacation. She stepped back into my doorway and told me her trip had been amazing and that she really wanted to tell me all about it but she didn't feel comfortable talking about it at the office. She then asked me if I would come over to her house one afternoon, after work, for a glass of wine, so she could tell me everything. The fact that she wanted me to come to her house to talk about her trip struck me as very odd, even a little mysterious. I couldn't understand why she would feel uncomfortable talking about her trip at the office. For some reason, I agreed to go by her house, but I asked her to tell me why she felt uncomfortable discussing her vacation at the office. Unexpectedly, Terri began to tear up and said it was just very personal. I couldn't help myself and I began to push her to tell me something, because I couldn't understand her tears. She then asked me if she could step into my office and close the door. She was still fighting back more tears so I motioned for her to come in and invited her to sit down. Within a few minutes, Terri was sitting across from my desk and telling me the intimate details of her trip. During the next three hours, I listened to Terri tell me story after story of miraculous things she had witnessed in a tiny village in Yugoslavia by the name of Medjugorje (pronounced Med-ju-gor-ria) and how these experiences had renewed her faith in a powerful way.

I was stunned. Prior to this, my relationship with Terri could only be described as casual. We worked together and had enjoyed a variety of social gatherings, usually revolving around the radio station. She was one of my employees and someone I had even struggled with a few times. I liked Terri but during this time I didn't view her as someone who was very serious or particularly committed to her work. I certainly did not view her as religious and I had no idea she had been raised Catholic. My impression of Terri was that she was a fun person but quite use to having things her own way. The Terri who was sitting in my office was different and I could see it immediately. She was more serious than I had ever seen her before and it was obvious something profound had happened to her.

Trust in the LORD with all your heart and
do not lean on your own understanding.
In all your ways acknowledge Him, and
He will make your paths straight.

Proverb 3:5-6
New American Standard Bible

Chapter 3

Three Hours That Changed My Life

JUDY

*T*he things Terri shared with me during the next three hours, behind my office door, could be a book itself. I can't remember exactly how she began, but I had never heard Terri talk with such purpose before. I listened intently as she described the events she and others had witnessed while in this remote village of Medjugorje. Terri told me that, shortly after she had arrived in Medjugorje, she had begun to feel a heaviness come over her. She described this as feeling the weight of her own life and how she had been living it. Although she was brought up in the Catholic Church, she had not been to confession in years and she had suddenly found herself wanting to talk to a priest and go to confession. I was not Catholic and the idea of needing a priest to confess your sins was foreign to me, but I could relate to the heaviness she was describing. She decided to go inside the church there to see if she could find a priest to hear her confession. While inside the church waiting on a priest, a very old peasant woman came in and sat down beside her. Terri described her as a very old woman, but she had been struck by how blue and young her eyes were. Terri was also struck by how kind and full of love this old woman was. The woman patted Terri on her knee and told her that she need not feel so burdened and that God knew of her sins and that He had already forgiven her. Terri described how her heaviness lifted from hearing these words and her immediate need for confession went away. After this occurrence, Terri had walked outside of the church and was standing in the court yard when she looked up at the clear blue sky. She described how, suddenly, the sky began turning blood red and how this sight had caused her to fall to her knees, right there in the middle of the day, in front of the church- in front of everyone. Terri continued to tell me many amazing things that she and the others traveling with her had witnessed during their week in Medjugorje.

At one point, Terri began to tell me about a mountain called Mt. Krizevac that was located on the outskirts of the village. On top of this mountain the villagers had erected a large cement cross. Almost everyone who traveled to Medjugorje climbed this treacherous mountain. She described the large numbers of people, from all over the world, which had climbed up the rocky path stopping along the way to pray at carved stones. These stones depicted the events that hap-

pened to Jesus on His way to His death on the Cross. She also described the local peasants who would walk up to the cross barefoot to further identify with Christ's suffering. As she was describing all of this I stopped her in complete astonishment, as I suddenly recalled my dream. Terri was describing, in detail, what I had seen in my dream during the week she was there. I had forgotten about this dream until now and, suddenly, something quickened in my heart and I knew exactly what I had seen in my dream. The dream was much more significant to me now and became more like a vision of what was going on in Medjugorje than a dream. I could hardly contain myself anymore. I began to tear up, still not understanding what all this really meant for me. I stopped Terri from talking and shared with her my dream about all the feet climbing a stony mountain with thorn bushes. She said that it accurately portrayed exactly what she witnessed there. As Terri continued to reveal more and more of her experiences in Medjugorje, I listened in amazement and awe. I could hardly believe what I was hearing, even though she had not yet told me the most meaningful of all her experiences- at least for me.

It was late one evening, Terri, her mother, her mother's friend Lois and two of Lois's daughters were talking about all the events of the week. Terri and Lois's daughters, Mary and Karen, had decided to take a walk into the village toward the Church there called St. James. As they walked up to the Church courtyard, Mary had felt a strong urge to be in the church, not just inside the church, but in a specific room inside the church which was to the right of the altar. When they approached the church's front doors, they were greeted by a couple of nuns who were cleaning up inside. The nuns told them they were sorry but they had to lock up because it was so late. Once they had locked the doors, Mary began to cry inconsolably. When Terri and Karen had asked what was wrong, she said that she knew she needed to be in the room to the right of the altar. Karen and Terri tried to console her and suggested that maybe they should go around the building, where the outside wall to this room was located. Once there, they noticed a window with a bench underneath it. This window appeared to be the one that looked into the room that Mary had felt drawn to.

Karen and Terri stood up on the bench and peered into the window, while Mary sat on the bench still in tears. According to Terri, as she and Karen were peering into the room, they noticed a statue of the Virgin Mary in the corner of this room. Within just a few minutes, the room began to fill up with what looked like a cloud and from out of the cloud the Virgin Mary appeared to them. They immediately called for Mary to get up and look. The three of them stood there in amazed silence as the Virgin Mary began to speak to them. Terri said they did not hear her audibly with their natural ear, but they *heard her clearly in words spoken silently, but directly, to their hearts and souls. First, she thanked them for coming and told them that it made her very happy to see her children from the West. She told them she was very worried about her children in the West because they had forgotten how much God had blessed them. The Virgin Mary said that her children in the West had begun to think that all their riches were of themselves and many had forgotten about God. She said that she had brought her Son into the world as a child but she was now appearing to draw people back to Him, while there was still time. After she spoke these words to all of them, Terri was given an individual message. It was here that Terri told me the Virgin Mary had presented her with a special mission. She requested that Terri come back to Medjugorje during a specific week in August. She was not to come back alone but she was to ask seven people to come back with her and the Virgin Mary presented her with each of their names. Terri said that she had told the Virgin Mary that she was concerned these people would not believe her and that they might not come. The Virgin Mary answered by telling Terri that this was not to concern her because she was simply to deliver the message. As Terri was telling me this she became very quiet and began to cry. Looking at me intently for a few seconds, trying to hold back her tears, she said, "Judy....she gave me your name."*

I don't remember what I said immediately, but my mind instantly recalled my prayer - the one I had written down on April 17th, just one month before this. "God, if You want me, You are going to have to come down here and show me, because I'm trying and I'm tired." Then I remembered the prayer Bob had prayed for me that day in his office, "Father, show Judy that you are real and send her a friend with whom she can share her faith."

My heart almost burst with emotions as tears filled up my eyes. I don't know if anyone can imagine what it felt like for me to hear these words from Terri's mouth. Instantly things seemed clear and the doubting in my heart was erased; there was only a knowing in my spirit that I can't explain and I felt no confusion. One thing I knew for certain: I knew I would be going to Medjugorje in August, even if I didn't know how. Unexpectedly, many parts of a puzzle were coming together for me and a picture was beginning to materialize. My questions and doubts were gone. I really didn't need to go to Medjugorje to "know" that God was real anymore. Still, I wanted to go because I had just been asked by the Blessed Virgin Mary herself, and that was an invitation I was not going to ignore.

Three hours had gone by while Terri and I had been talking in my office behind a closed door. Oddly enough, we had not been interrupted once. When we finally opened the door and walked out, almost everyone in the office had already gone home. Somehow, I managed to walk to my car, in a daze of wonderment, and drove myself home. On the way home, I considered how I was going to tell Don everything that Terri had just told me. I had no idea how he would react. At the moment it didn't seem to matter because I knew my prayers had been heard and I knew that God existed. I knew Jesus was real and, even more personal for me - His mother had called me by my name and had offered me a personal invitation.

So faith comes from hearing, that is, hearing the Good News about Christ.

Romans 10:17
New Living Translation

Chapter 4

The Conversation

DON

Have you ever seen "that look" on someone's face? If you've known someone for a period of years, the unspoken word can be accompanied by a look or expression and you just know something's up. That's how it was when Judy walked through the door. I could tell just by the look on her face that something had happened. She seemed a bit excited, but also apprehensive, as she came over to me and said with a sense of urgency in her voice, "I've got to talk to you." "What about?" I had asked spontaneously. All she said was, "Not right now." I knew that she meant not in front of Blake. Blake was my 10 year old, from my previous marriage, and he was sitting in the living area waiting for dinner. When Judy does not answer right away, I know what we have to talk about requires sitting down and that it's very important to her.

The topic of highest priority for months had been our desire to start a family. My immediate thought was that Judy was pregnant again and I wasn't sure how I was going to react to this. She had just started to heal from the last miscarriage and I knew how sad she had been afterwards. I wasn't sure if I should be happy or more worried about her. I "checked in with myself" because I knew how important my reaction would be to her and, worried or not, I wanted to respond the right way. All through dinner I was thinking about what I should say and I kept telling myself to be positive and supportive no matter what direction the conversation took. We rushed through dinner and I got Blake distracted in his bedroom. When I came back into the living room, Judy was patiently waiting and sitting there on the couch with "that look." So, I went over, sat down and said "What's up?" feeling pretty sure that I already knew.

The first thing out of Judy's mouth was, "You're not going to believe the conversation I had with Terri this afternoon." This was not what I was expecting and it seemed to come from out of nowhere. I was still preparing myself to hear that Judy was pregnant and trying to figure out what this had to do with Terri. My assumption that Judy was pregnant was all wrong. I don't remember if I was more disappointed or relieved, but I wasn't quite sure what could be so interesting about a conversation with Terri. Judy had mentioned to me a few weeks back something about Terri going to Yugoslavia, but I thought the whole thing was a little bizarre. As Judy began to relay some of the things Terri had told her, I remembered hearing something about this village called Medjugorje on one of the '60 Minutes' programs, sometime before. My memory of the story involved some children who had claimed to see the Virgin Mary. It had been so long ago I barely remembered any of the details. A story that I found vaguely interesting in the past had found its way into my living room, only now it was coming from someone who claimed to have had a first-hand experience there. I was still thinking of Terri's trip in terms of a vacation. The idea of anyone choosing to spend vacation time going to a small rural village, in a communist country, for something like this, seemed a little "out there" to me. I had gotten to know Terri, along with many of the people in Judy's office. I had never thought of her as someone who was religious, or even spiritual, and I found that idea of her a bit of a challenge. While very likeable, Terri always seemed quite materialistic and I had imagined her vacationing more on the French Riviera than someone interested in going on a religious pilgrimage. I couldn't imagine why Terri, or anyone, would choose to spend their time doing this and I had accepted Judy's explanation that she had gone out of an obligation, rather than anything else.

As Judy continued with the story she said, "Don, you are not going to believe what happened to Terri on her trip." I could see she really wanted to talk about this but I wasn't interested in a long conversation now that I realized the topic. I had a lot of work to wrap up before the next day, so I did what I often did when I was distracted. I looked at my watch and asked her how long it was going to take. So often when Judy wanted to talk, she would need to give all the background and details. I was too impatient for that and I just wanted her to get to the point that had something to do with either her, me or us. My impatience was upsetting to her and she said, "No, Don, this is important!" There was something in her tone and her face that told me it was and that I needed to listen.

As Judy began to tell me everything, including all the background, I tried to listen as attentively as I could, but I grew very distracted and impatient. I wanted to know where this was going. There were times my thoughts would drift off thinking about what she was saying. I was really trying to keep focused and not let a single thought cause me to drift too far away from the continuity of the events as they began to unfold. I remained silent but my thoughts were racing somewhere in between "this is unimaginable," to "is it even remotely possible that any of this could be true?" Much of what Judy was telling me was also challenging to my belief system. If it had been anyone else, besides Judy, sitting here telling me this, I am sure I would have thought this story was the product of "too much juice of the vines" during someone's vacation. I wasn't sure what I really thought, but Judy had always been a level headed person and I could see she had confidence in what she had been told. I had never known Judy to be flighty and I considered her to be someone with both feet planted squarely on the ground. Listening to her speak with so much assurance was somewhat convincing. Nevertheless, when Judy got to the part about the Virgin Mary actually speaking to Terri, Karen and Mary I had a hard time keeping a straight face. I knew better than to laugh because I knew Judy was being very sincere- but still!!! None of this seemed possible, especially to a "Cradle Baptist." I did not laugh, but I was having a hard time holding back my nervous smile. The conversation became increasingly uncomfortable and I could not find a place in my logical thought process where any of this could fit in.

To think the Virgin Mary might be appearing to six children somewhere far away was one thing, but to accept that she actually spoke to someone I knew was stretching me way beyond my perception of reality. Judy continued to tell me that the Virgin Mary had given Terri seven names of individuals that she was to bring back to Medjugorje in August, just three months away. All of these thoughts were swirling around in my head and I don't think Judy even noticed the smile I was still nervously trying to hide. This seemed completely impossible to me. My impulse to smile or laugh was immediately halted when I began to see tears well up in Judy's eyes and watched a single tear roll down her cheek. For the first time, I think I realized what all this indicated to Judy and I wanted to reach out to her but I saw her draw up as if she was trying to embolden herself. Just as I was about to reach out to her, she pulled back, straightened her back and lifted her head. Holding back her tears, Judy dropped the bomb on me when she told me one of the names given to Terri had been hers. I couldn't say a word. I mean, I was already feeling so uneasy with all of this and now Judy was sitting there telling me the Virgin Mary, the mother of Christ, had asked for her, by name, through one of her co-workers. I didn't know what to think or say. I was looking at Judy and there seemed to be no doubt in her, only assurance and joy, as she believed that God was in the midst of all this and that he had heard her prayer. To give her confirmation, he had sent her a vision, in a dream, of the things that were to come. I couldn't think of a word to say, so I simply surprised myself by softly asking, "What are you going to do?" It was a stretch to even ask the obvious question. "Are you going?" Judy answered with an unwavering "Yes!" That was not the answer I was hoping for. I was met with the strangest feeling. I didn't know why but, for some reason, I felt personally threatened by all of this, but now was not the time to say anything.

> By faith Abraham, when he was called,
> obeyed by going out to a place which he
> was to receive for an inheritance; and, by
> faith, he went out not knowing
> where he was going.
>
> Hebrew 11:18
> New American Standard Bible

Chapter 5

Conflicts, Confusion and Uncertainties

JUDY

*T*he following weeks and months leading up to the August 10th departure date was filled with conflicts between Don and me. The tension between us was growing day by day and I wasn't exactly sure why. I knew Don was very unsettled by all of this and the idea of going on a trip to a communist country was compounding things. It was quite obvious from all of Don's little digs, all of his questions and the million reasons he continuously gave for not wanting us to go. There were many times I really didn't think he would be going with me. Then he would change his mind and say he might go because he didn't want me to go by myself. As far as I was concerned, I was at complete peace - inwardly anyway. Even still, the arguments were getting to me and it was difficult to understand the exact source. There seemed to be much more going on with Don than met the eye.

Don has a way of making fun of things if they make him uncomfortable. Instead of just coming out and saying- "This makes me uneasy"- he makes jokes. This was the case one afternoon when the radio station was doing a remote broadcast at Hooters. It was in the afternoon, after work, and the staff from the radio station was there enjoying the nice weather out on Hooters' porch. Don stopped by to have a beer with everyone and upon seeing Terri there he asked her, quite jokingly, in front of everyone if she only drank "gold" beer now. He was making a reference to the fact that she had told me her rosary chain had turned a golden color while in Medjugorje. Terri was good spirited about it and laughed, but it was Don's way of saying-"This is crazy to me!"

Don and I had another scheduled appointment with Bob coming up and I could hardly wait to share everything that had transpired since our last meeting and his prayer. As with the last appointment, Don and I were both supposed to be there together and once again Don had forgotten. I was beginning to get concerned about how often Don seemed to be forgetting things. Just that morning, he had said he would be there because he wanted to talk to Bob about "this trip." To be honest, I was relieved he did not show up. I wanted a chance to tell Bob what had happened and get his reaction first. Don *wanted to talk about his opposition to going to Medjugorje and I knew that conversation would take up most of the entire hour. Once it was apparent that Don was not coming, I began to tell Bob everything that was going on. The whole hour was filled with me telling him all that had happened to Terri and the message she had brought back to me. We both marveled at how, just two weeks earlier, Bob had prayed that God would show me He was real and place someone in my path that would help me in my search for answers. This sure seemed like an answer to that prayer, but it was so much more than that. Bob had heard of Medjugorje and he knew people who had gone there before. He really didn't say anything overly positive or negative about it. I sensed his reaction was similar to mine -amazement, awe and simply open to seeing what God was doing and where He was leading. At the end of our meeting, Bob asked me how Don felt about this and if he was going to go with me. I answered I wasn't sure and that I knew he was really struggling with all of it. I explained that it had become a major source of conflict between us. This time, Bob simply encouraged me to pray about it. I could sense Bob had also been moved by the things I had told him. As I began to write him a check for our session, I inwardly amused myself by thinking that Bob should be paying me for this one.*

As we got closer and closer to our departure date, Don and I continued to argue about one thing or another. He began to remind me that we had planned on taking a trip to the islands for our one year anniversary in August. He was thinking maybe we would even go back to Bermuda where we had gone on our honeymoon. It had been a wonderful honeymoon and we both had loved the idea of a chance to go back. He was not very happy that this trip to Yugoslavia was going to put an end to that idea or any other vacation idea he might have. There was no way we could afford two trips so close together. He began to act resentfully and made comments that he really wasn't excited about spending our first anniversary in a communist country with a bunch of "beehived hairdoed ladies" - making reference to his perceptions of what religious women looked like.

One day Don asked me a rather odd question out of the blue. He wanted to know if the Virgin Mary had asked for Judy Bailey or if she had asked for Judy Powell, my maiden name. I really didn't know and I hadn't thought to ask because it wasn't important to me. For some reason, this seemed to be important to Don. It would only be much later on before I would begin to understand the reason behind this rather odd and random question.

Another month flew by and it was getting very close to departure. It was also time for us to meet with Bob again. This time Don made it, and I was really glad because the tension was at an all-time high between us. I wasn't sure if Don was actually going to go. Once we were both sitting in Bob's office many of Don's real concerns began to come out in the open. He made it clear that he wasn't sure he was going or why he should go. His name hadn't been given to Terri by the Virgin Mary. On the other hand, he didn't want me to go without him. He was very concerned about what might happen. He was worried I might come back one of those "religious" women he had a hard time relating to. He wasn't even sure he would still want to be married to me if I came back like that. To be truthful, I wasn't sure he wanted to be married to me even right then. It was obvious all of this was creating incredible stress for him. He hadn't bargained for any of this when we got married and he wanted to just stop all this nonsense and go to Bermuda, not Medjugorje.

It was Bob, in his kind and gentle way, which told Don he had heard of Medjugorje and that he actually knew people who had gone there. He also said something to Don that seemed to give him perhaps a different outlook about everything that was going on between us. He spoke in a way that I know surprised Don. I suspect Don went to our meeting with Bob looking for support and hoping Bob would back him up and talk some sense into me. Instead Bob spoke to him from another perspective. He told Don many of the people he knew who had gone to Medjugorje had also encountered inner conflicts about going as well as other difficulties before leaving for Medjugorje. Many obstacles had been thrown in front of them that they had perceived to be a threat to their trip. Most felt something strong was calling them to Medjugorje, but that another force was working hard to prevent it from happening. Here was Bob, someone Don had known for a long time and someone he really respected, asking him to question why he was fighting this so hard. Bob told Don that, if everything inside him was fighting this trip, maybe he should pay attention to what that might be. Bob suggested that maybe he should just go and see, expecting nothing. Something in that made practical sense to Don and he slowly began to surrender towards making the trip with me.

DON

Over the following days, I continued to try and come to terms with this trip we were about to take. I had agreed to go but now I was beginning to question again why. I still really did not want to go. After talking with Bob I had, however, begun to get a little intrigued about it, if nothing else. It may have been simple curiosity to see if there was anything to this. My concept of God, faith or religion simply would not embrace any of this as a reality. There was still something gnawing at my core. My fears were that this somehow could end up ruining our marriage. I didn't want things to change. I felt like my life had been invaded by Terri coming back with this strange message that Judy was supposed to go to Medjugorje the exact week of our one year anniversary. I felt unfairly caught between my own personal desires and my certain damning if I didn't go along. I knew I had a choice. I didn't have to go, but I did have to make a choice. The timing of this really made me angry and I wanted to know why we had to go now? Was it so wrong that I wanted to go on a real vacation with my wife? I wanted to go somewhere where we could lay out in the sun, eat delicious food, drink and dance in the evenings. I needed the break and we needed to spend some quality time together, living the good life. This had been a tough first year for us with some heartbreaking disappointments and this is what I thought we really needed. The idea of spending an entire week in a remote, rural village, compared to a trip back to Bermuda, offered absolutely no inspiration for me. The thought of being trapped in an environment I was so much at odds with seemed beyond what I thought I could endure. The very thought of a week like this made me feel trapped, even claustrophobic. I had a hard time sitting in church for more than a half hour, so how was I supposed to handle an entire week like this? The idea I might be sequestered with possibly charismatic Christians for a week, with no means of an escape, felt like a horrifying nightmare. No doubt, it certainly was a waste of valuable vacation time. I had to laugh at the thought of this just to keep myself sane.

I always saw in Judy a good spirit and an honest person who was dedicated to doing what she thought was right. There was nothing phony about her. She was definitely much more of a seeker than me. I would find her journaling her thoughts and talking about our responsibilities as people to each other. She was always asking questions and thinking about things I was uncomfortable with. She seemed to expect much more of God than I did. She actually expected He would somehow be involved in our lives in a personal way. I don't think I was comfortable with the idea of God being so close and knowing all the things I might be thinking some of the time. I was not even taught to think about having some kind of an ongoing relationship with a living God. My ideas of God were pretty basic. I believed God was somewhere in heaven and we were here on earth and one day we would see him, if we hadn't done anything too horrible. Somehow, I must have missed the Sunday School lesson about needing to have a relationship with Him. If someone did say something like that, I was sure they were speaking metaphorically. For me, it was a hypothesis never really tested.

There was actually one point in my life when I thought I was beginning to get close to God and experience what

Judy referred to as a spiritual connection. It happened while attending a Billy Graham meeting. Toward the end of the meeting, an event happened that squelched this process and left me feeling a deep separation from God. In fact, I was sure that, while it might be possible for others to connect with God, it would never be possible for me. It was a very disturbing experience but, once I believed this, my heart hardened, as far as God was concerned. I had never shared with anyone what happened there, but it had left me with no hope of a spiritual life. I had kept this experience a well-protected secret for years. Because of this experience, I was sure that God didn't listen to my prayers. From that moment on, I resolved to depend on myself, not God, for whatever I needed or wanted to accomplish. It had been a very long time since I had allowed my memory to go back to that place. I saw no need in going back there now, so I pushed it aside like always.

Right up to the time for us to go, I continued to battle with whatever it was that was telling me not to go. There was a powerful grip holding me and giving me a million reasons why I shouldn't go and, more importantly, why "we" shouldn't go. All of those reasons continuously kept rolling over in my mind. One, we didn't need to waste our money on this. Two, this was our one year anniversary for crying out loud! Three, it wasn't fair that I was going to miss out on a relaxing vacation that we needed. Four, if my back went out again I would be in a remote location far away from any good doctors. Even if I couldn't admit it to myself or anyone else, the biggest grip on me for not wanting to go had something to do with the memory of that night at the Billy Graham meeting. Additionally, it struck me as curious that Judy was asked to go the week of August the 10th. If the Virgin Mary knew her name, I was certain that she also knew her wedding anniversary. It felt like she was personally messing with me. The inner turmoil I was experiencing about this trip was overwhelming. I wanted to bolt and say "I'm done with this, I'm out of here!"

I could not imagine what I was going to have in common with all these religious people. In my opinion, all "overly religious" people had a certain degree of phoniness about them that I didn't trust. Most likely I received this prejudice from my father, who held this same opinion. My Dad was a fair and very honest man, but he was given to some very strong opinions that he more often should have kept to himself. One of these strong opinions involved overly religious people. One of his favorite sayings was that "They did a lot of shouting on Sunday and a lot of sinning on Monday." Mother, on the other hand, had made sure we attended church. I had also been active in the youth group and attended Vacation Bible School just like Judy. Still, I managed to be influenced by the exploits of several of the older boys in our community, and at an early age I had a front seat to a very worldly side of life. To me, this was the "real world" and these religious people were just "acting" all pious.

Judy's world growing up was different. In her opinion, all these men of worldly exploits were the imposters and she didn't believe half of what they said they did. We would often argue about who had the most correct view of the "real" world. For the most part, Judy was allowed to grow up in a protected environment, with both parents committed to a Christian way of life. Her Christian upbringing was not something she wore on her sleeve, but it was something that was ingrained in her being. This worked for me, because I never saw Judy as overly religious or pious. Judy was a lot of fun and she knew how to have a good time. She could laugh at an off-colored joke without getting uptight. She had lots of friends and people really liked her. Judy was optimistic and seemed to find fun in anything she did. Besides being in love with her, I liked her for the same reasons everybody else did and I felt really fortunate to have her as my wife. Judy had once told me she had been attracted to me because I was different from most of the other men she had dated. She had witnessed me with my son and saw me as a responsible and caring father. I was seven years older than her and, when we met, I had my own business. She viewed me as a man who had matured beyond boyish ways. Somehow, I had managed to disguise a lot of my cynicism from her, because I knew she would not be impressed. Even still, Judy and I were compatible in many areas. Our biggest difference was, in a word, joy. It was something that seemed so natural to her and yet it was so strange to me. I just could not go to that place of joy she could. I marveled at how she seemed to put her trust in God. I dismissed most of this and thought, "If this works for her, then fine." I just didn't get it.

This last year had been tough on Judy. The miscarriages and the fear that she would never have a child had caused her deep pain and disappointment. Somehow, I feared a portion of her disappointment was in me, even though she never verbalized it. When it came to the subject of God, I could sense something unfulfilled in her about me. I knew Judy thought I was a good person, even if I was a bit rough around the edges, but I also knew it was her desire for me to be closer to God. Listening to some of the things she did say, I knew she believed this would make us closer too. Judy had prayed for God to save each child, but she lost them anyway. She told me she had started to question her faith. It was obvious she had counted on God and she had been severely disappointed. From my perspective, I did not think

God had so much let her down but rather she just expected too much from Him. Based on my experience, I believed you had to rely on yourself and not God. That old rule of "If it's to be, it's up to me" had been taught to me all my life. When the going gets tough, the tough get going. My way of handling things was to just get up and brush yourself off. During this time, there was no way I could get Judy on board through my way of handling things. She was looking inward and upward and trying to figure out why God had closed His ears to her. I somewhat blamed myself that much of Judy's pain was because I could not understand or relate to her feelings in all of this. Now, here we were not yet a full year into our marriage and the strength of our marriage was being tested in a big way.

During this same time period, I had another memory that was haunting me as well. It was something that had happened a little over a year before Judy and I had gotten married. I was struggling with the thought that there might be a connection between what was going on now and what had happened to me then. I had never been able to make sense of what had happened to me until now. The most uncomfortable thing was that it had a real parallel to Judy's story. One afternoon, I had experienced a major confrontation with some members of my family. The blow up had been building for a very long time. The extent of this confrontation had really gotten to me and I was feeling the full force of my anger and frustration towards them. There was nothing in me but the intensity of my anger and it was so great that I knew I had to get away from everyone before I exploded. I had jumped into my truck and started driving without any thought of where I was going. All I knew was I had to get away. At some point, I ended up driving north of town, (in Tallahassee) on Live Oak Plantation Road. I had never felt this kind of intense rage and I couldn't understand why things had to be the way they were with my family. I felt nothing but anger and resentment and I was yelling at the top of my voice and banging on the steering wheel. I wanted to hit something. There wasn't one good thought running through my mind at the time. In the midst of all this anger and rage I heard a voice, coming from inside my truck, say very loud and clear, "GIVE IT UP!" It startled me to the point that I slammed on the brakes, pulled off the road, popped off my seat belt and turned defiantly to see who was there. My heart was pounding and adrenalin was racing so fast I felt the pressure rise in my ear drums, and then it was over. There was no one there, nothing, but I know I heard the words and they were crystal clear and audible. The words spoke directly to my anger and to everything I was feeling. These were three words given to me to let me know I had to let this anger with my family go before it destroyed me and all my relationships. When I heard those words, every emotion I had been bottling up just cried out, "Oh God! Help Me! Please God; please take this horrible pain from me." It was a natural and instinctive cry that came without any forethought. It came right from the deep pain and I believe, for one moment, my soul took over and I spoke to God without thinking, directly from my heart.

Over the last few weeks this incident kept coming up in my mind. I had almost forgotten about it. I had forgotten that, while in my own distress, I too had actually done like Judy and called on a higher authority to fix what I couldn't.

I don't know how long I sat there on the side of Live Oak Plantation Road that afternoon. It was typically a busy road but I don't remember any cars passing by except one. At this exact moment, Judy, who was supposed to be at work, just happened to drive by. I couldn't believe it when she pulled off the road behind me. I got out of the truck, walked to her car, opened the door and sat down in the passenger's seat. Unlike the incident that happened with Billy Graham, this time I told Judy everything. That day I drove home alone with my thoughts on what had just occurred. I wanted to argue with myself about where this voice had originated from. I tried to rationalize it. Was it God or just my subconscious knowledge all along telling me what I knew I needed to do? Somehow, I just could not believe my mind alone could ever generate such clarity of thought in three words, not to the point that it seemed audible. Then I realized that my own thoughts had never startled me before. The voice had come from outside of me, but it was still too much to truly comprehend.

Now, as I was recalling what had happened on Live Oak Plantation Road, a year earlier, I wondered if maybe it was possible that God could step in when we needed His help the most. Maybe what was going on with Judy was an answer to her prayer. Maybe I shouldn't fight this so hard. I don't know why, but I finally decided after much going back and forth, to take Bob's advice and "Just go, expecting nothing."

While from behind, a voice shall sound in your ears: "This is the way; walk in it"

Isaiah 30:21a
The New American Bible

Chapter 6

Our First Gathering

JUDY

*T*he airline tickets were finally purchased and our pass-
ports were ready. As far as I knew, Don, while maybe
not at peace with all of this, had at least now officially
resigned himself to go. We would be traveling with Terri
and her mother, Barbara, as well as her friend Lois and two
of Lois's daughters, Linda and Mary. Altogether, there was
going to be twenty-one people in our travel group. Thirteen
of the twenty-one were from Tallahassee. Four of the seven
people that the Virgin Mary had asked Terri to deliver the
message to decided to answer "the call" and go. For me, there
was only one concern now. One of the names Terri had been
given was the husband of one of my employees, who was also
in the sales department. He had decided to go and, of course,
his wife wanted to go with him. There was no way I was

going to stand in the way of someone going on a pilgrimage like this. This meant there would be three of us from the sales department away at the same time "on a pilgrimage" in a foreign country: myself, and two of my sales people. To say this might appear a little strange to most people, especially those in a professional and competitive business where the bottom line and quotas were more important than anything else, is putting it mildly. I was fortunate, during this time, to have had an understanding boss, but I had no idea what our new owners were going to be like or when they might be popping in.

When someone purchases a radio station they have to wait for the FCC to approve the transfer of the license. Typically, it is difficult to determine the exact time frame for processing the paper work for this approval. The paper work could pile up at the FCC office for what would seem like an eternity. Then again, it could go through rather quickly. We all expected this sale would go through fairly quickly and I had no way of knowing when the new owners would be actually taking over the operation. I could only imagine how this might look to them. I could hear the questions they would ask my boss, Mark Halverson. "Now, where did you say your sales manager was? And she is with two of your key sales people over there? And tell me again why three people in the sales department are in Yugoslavia?" I was sure this would *be the end of my career if they ended up taking over the radio station while we were gone. I was sure they would label me some kind of a religious nut, not to mention an irresponsible sales manager, for taking three of us out of the department at the same time. I knew this was the kind of first impression that might end up costing me my job. It didn't matter. The die was cast and we were all going. I only hoped God would take care of this situation and keep the ownership transfer from going through until we were all back at work. Little did I know, He had already taken care of everything. Shortly after our return, I would meet our new owner, Jesus Soto, from Puerto Rico, and learn he and his family were devout Catholics. His wife would be very familiar with Medjugorje and interested in hearing every detail concerning our trip.*

About two weeks before we were to leave, our travel agent arranged for all of us to meet at Lois's house. This was the first time we were to meet the others who would be traveling with us. It was an interesting group of all ages, young and old, singles and married. As soon as we all gathered in Lois's family room, we learned this was more than a meeting about our itinerary or to talk about what we should carry with us. We opened the gathering in prayer and soon those who had previously traveled to Medjugorje began to tell us about some of the hardships that often accompanied people who had decided to make the journey to Medjugorje. Many people had reported things such as sicknesses, other ailments and family emergencies. Many thought they were going to have to cancel their trip, but as soon as they got on the plane these issues either went away or lessened. This sounded very similar to some of the stories that Bob tried to tell Don he had heard as well. As our travel agent talked to us, she kept referring to people who had traveled to Medjugorje as pilgrims and the trip as a pilgrimage. I looked over at Don and could feel him tightening up and getting uncomfortable. I could tell he was having a hard time relating to any of the conversation and I prayed he would not start grilling them with questions the way he had done me. After giving us an idea of what our itinerary would be, as well as giving us suggestions on what to take and what not to take, we were then asked if we had any questions. Several people had questions like: "Will we be able to meet the visionaries?" or "What kind of gifts should we take our host family?", or "Will we get to hear Fr. Jozo speak?" and, "Is there an English speaking Mass?" These were the kinds of questions from those interested in seeing, touching and meeting as many people as they could that were associated with everything going on in Medjugorje. Don had a list of questions too. He asked things like: "Will we have air conditioning?"; "Will we be able to buy conveniences like toothpaste or snacks?"; "Are there doctors in Medjugorje?"; "Do they have restaurants?" These questions were more con-

venience-type questions and I could tell by looking at the faces of some in the group that they were wondering who this person was. I got the look of..."Oh, I understand, you're dragging your husband along."

The meeting lasted about an hour. Don and I had so much to do before we left and I think this was a blessing in disguise. During this time, we had decided to scratch our plans to build a house and instead move into one of Don's spec homes. We had to be in our new home before we left, in order to get Blake in the school he needed to be in. We were rushing to pick out appliances, wallpaper, paint colors and flooring. We were going to have to pack up the house we were currently in and get ready for a move across town. By the time we would return home from Medjugorje, Blake would already be back in school, so we also had to shop for his school clothes and supplies. To say it was a bit overwhelming is putting it mildly, but still, I had such an inner peace. The busyness served the purpose of keeping us from having to think anything more about the trip.

We made the move and unloaded all of our belongings into our new home the day before we were to leave. The only thing we had time to put together was our bed so we would have a place to sleep. Our flight was out of Jacksonville, FL so the following day we drove away from our new home with everything still in boxes. Once we arrived in Jacksonville, we met several people traveling in our group from Tallahassee at a hotel near the airport where we spent the night before our flight out early the next morning.

Blessed are those whose strength is in you, whose hearts are set on a pilgrimage.

Psalms 84:5

New International Version

Chapter 7

The Journey Begins

JUDY

*A*ugust 10*th,* 1990; the trip was finally happening. There were others traveling with us that we were to meet once we arrived at JFK, in New York. Our flight out of Jacksonville had a brief scheduled stop in Baltimore. While waiting for others to board the plane, there was an announcement that our plane would not be allowed to take off immediately due to bad weather conditions in New York. This delay caused us to be severely late getting into JFK. We were concerned that we would not be able to meet the others waiting on us there or make our connecting flight to Dubrovnik. To make matters worse, the shuttle that was transporting us to another area of the airport had at least a dozen or more stops before getting to our terminal. When we finally arrived at our stop everyone jumped off and started running through the airport as fast as we possibly could. The airline agents were closing the door as the first ones in our group arrived at the gate. They told the attendant that there were thirteen in our group and begged them to hold up the plane. We all made it through, but somehow, Don and I ended up being the last ones to board this massive DC 10. Because of our delay, we ended up with seats in the very last row of the plane. The whole ordeal had been stressful to say the least. As we settled down in our seats, we soon began to realize just what this delay had cost us.

This was in 1990, before the smoking bans on planes, and there were many Europeans traveling on this trans-continental flight. I had no idea Europeans liked to smoke so much. It seemed like almost everyone on this flight was a smoker and their favorite cigarettes were strong, unfiltered tobacco. To make matters worse, the last six rows in the back of the plane, were designated for smokers only. Here we were, sitting in the back of the plane, in the smoking section that was obviously not large enough to accommodate all the smokers on the flight. Not being smokers ourselves, we quickly realized we were in trouble because, before we lifted off, everyone in our section started lighting up. Within a few minutes, an additional 10 to 15 other people made their way to the back of the plane, stood over our seats and joined in the "smoke-fest". This was the beginning of a continuous flow of people throughout the entire flight, as one by one a new group of smokers would take their break. Don wasn't happy with any of this and I felt like I was turning green. At some point during the middle of the night, I could not stand it any longer. I grabbed my pillow and placed it over my face and stood up. The flight attendant, who earlier in the flight looked like she would slap your knuckles if you did something out of line (like ask for coffee at the wrong time) came by and asked me if I was going to be sick. I told her that I might and indicated the smoke was really getting to me. She didn't say a word and she just left. Within a few minutes, she returned to the back of the plane, tapped me on the shoulder and whispered for us to leave all our belongings and quietly follow her. Without saying another word to us, she discretely took us all the way to the front of the plane and into first class. She pointed to a couple of seats in the center section and gave us a fresh blanket and a couple of pillows and, with tremendous gratitude, we soon went to sleep in our large, comfortable, reclining leather chairs.

Fortunately, we were able to sleep through the night in our new comfort and we did not wake up until the flight attendants began waking everyone up in first class for breakfast. As Don and I stood up to stretch, we began looking around the first class cabin and we were shocked to find that at least six others traveling from Tallahassee, including Terri, had *also somehow made it up to first class during the night. All of us had been scattered throughout this massive plane and now eight of us were sitting in first class, due to the kindness of this rather large-framed airline stewardess that I had called "Broom Hilda" when we first got on the plane. I was beginning to feel like we were already receiving some of God's special graces as we made our way through the air toward Dubrovnik. As everyone began to wake up, one by one, all we could do was just quietly smile at each other over the special favor we had been given on this incredibly long flight. As soon as breakfast was over, the pilot announced that we were now flying over the White Cliffs of Dover. I could hardly believe we were already over England and approaching the European Continent. The flight took us over the Swiss Alps as we made our way to the ancient, fortified city of Dubrovnik.*

We finally arrived in Dubrovnik around noon local time. We de-boarded the plane and each of us made our way through customs only to learn that almost everyone's luggage, including ours, had not made the connecting flight out of JFK. Here we were, with no luggage, getting ready to board a bus that would take us three hours away from the airport into one of the most remote areas of the country. There would be no clothing stores and no Wal-Mart's to buy anything. The airport officials could not tell us where our luggage was or when we might expect it. The customs agents really were not into comforting us or addressing our concerns. They seemed only interested in getting us through customs as soon as possible so we would not hold up their line. We quickly gave them the information on how to contact us once our luggage arrived and they pushed us on through, showing little concern for our belongings. There was nothing we could do except hope and pray that our luggage, with all our clothes, would soon arrive.

Don was especially annoyed with losing our luggage. After hearing Terri talk about the long hike we would be taking up the mountain, with the sharp rocks, Don had purchased a new pair of hiking boots. Don was someone who always prided himself on having the best equipment and tools for every eventuality. There were a lot of "special things" we had purchased to help make our time in Medjugorje more comfortable. Don and I had lost luggage before on our travels and had learned a very valuable lesson. Due to that experience, we had decided to pack a change of clothes in each of our carry-on bags. Also, after that experience, I never went anywhere without carrying my toiletries, including my makeup, on board with me. Others in our group had checked everything in and had absolutely nothing but what they had on.

Once we made it through customs, we met our guide, Dragan, just outside the airport. We followed him to the bus that would take us on the next leg of our journey, the three hour winding drive from Dubrovnik into the tiny village of Medjugorje. Dragan was a very handsome young man, somewhere in his twenties, who lived in Medjugorje and who was well acquainted with the six visionaries. He was a wealth of information about Dubrovnik, as well as the history of his country and, of course, everything that had been going on in Medjugorje for the last nine years.

The city of Dubrovnik was beautiful, with its fortressed walls, and the drive along the Adriatic Sea, high above the cliffs, was breathtaking. At some points, we were so high above the ocean that photos we later looked at made viewers think we were in an airplane instead of a bus. We could look down on the beaches and people looked like small ants. The ocean was so clear, I could see to the bottom from my window seat. About an hour and a half into our drive, we stopped at a roadside cafe for lunch. Everyone was in a happy, expectant mood and I could feel the excitement growing in everyone as we chatted over lunch. It was here that we began to sense the difference between where we were now and back home. We asked for water and we got a small glass with no ice. When Don asked if he could have some ice, the waitress acted a little annoyed with him and when she came back she dropped one cube into his glass. Don looked at me and laughed. He could tell that he would not be very popular if he were to ask for just a little more ice. As we sat talking, I could sense Don was beginning to relax and I was pleased that he seemed to be enjoying everyone's conversation.

DON

With each passing moment, I was becoming a little more relaxed and comfortable with being here. Judy looked like she was in heaven and I saw her having fun in a way I had not seen in some time. I was still not sure what I was doing here, but for a change I was living in the moment and having a good time. In addition to the water, I had ordered a beer and was surprised to find that it, unlike the water, was ice cold. I was smiling at Judy and loving the look on her face. After lunch, we all got back on the bus for the final part of the drive. Once back on the road, one of the women in our group suggested that everyone pray a Rosary and this is the moment the five Protestants in our group began to feel like we were in an unfamiliar land, in more ways than one. This was the first time I had ever actually heard anyone praying the Rosary. I listened with some interest but continued looking out the window at the scenery, which began to change as we departed the coast line and headed inland. Now we were getting into rolling hills and a more rural area with lots of farmland. There were small white houses with red tile roofs scattered here and there, and I began to settle in for the balance of the three hour drive to Medjugorje.

JUDY

When everyone had finished praying, Terri reached across the aisle from me and asked me to look at her Rosary. The silver chain between the beads on the Rosary had indeed turned a rich golden color. She smiled at me and said that the closer we got to Medjugorje, the brighter the gold was becoming. I didn't know what to say, so I just smiled and shook my head. I showed the Rosary to Don and I could tell he didn't know what to make of this either. Things were starting to quiet down now, as everyone began anticipating our arrival. I sat quietly for much of the last hour, deep in my own thoughts. I remember the sun was getting lower in the sky and everything, including the houses, the trees and land seemed to have a surreal warm glow. I had no idea what I was getting myself into or what I was really expecting. To be honest, I don't think I was expecting anything in particular. Just because the Virgin Mary had appeared to Terri and just because so many in her group had experienced many miracles on their trip three months ago, it didn't mean it would happen to any of us on our trip. It sure didn't mean it would happen to me. I was O.K. with that. Somewhere in my heart I believed that maybe this had more to do with Don than me. He had so much trouble accepting what I believed to be going on. My prayers had already been answered. Don was the person with so much resistance about coming. There was something about this that made me believe he was going to get some answers here - even if he wasn't consciously looking for any. As I gazed out my window, looking at the mid-afternoon sun in the sky, I was experiencing tremendous peace. I was profoundly content. For once in my life, at this particular moment, I knew for sure that I was exactly where I was supposed to be. The pain of not knowing whether God cared for me had vanished; even the pain of the miscarriages had somehow disappeared. As I sat quietly on the bus, I began meditating on everything that had happened, treasuring this peaceful moment and the events that had brought me here in my heart.

**Then you will experience God's peace,
which exceeds anything we
can understand. His peace will guard
your hearts and minds as you live in
Christ Jesus.**

**Philippians 4:7
New Living Translation**

Chapter 8

Medjugorje Arrival

DON

The long bus ride was winding down and our guide, Dragan, informed us we would be arriving in Medjugorje within the next few minutes. The narrow two-lane road was beginning to get very congested and, as the bus approached the edge of town, the traffic came to an abrupt halt. For some reason, I had not expected to see this kind of congestion. The magnitude of what was going on here still had not settled in on me. I turned to Judy and asked her if she had realized that so many people were going to be here. She commented that Terri had told her that people came here from all over the world, but even she was surprised to actually see this many people traveling in at the same time. With the bus traveling so slowly, I think Dragan felt the need to explain what was going on to everyone. He stood up at the front of the bus, took the microphone in his hand and began to explain that this was actually a very special week in Medjugorje. He continued to explain that the crowds would be even larger, as more pilgrims would be coming in to celebrate the Feast of the Assumption of the Virgin Mary on August 15th. As a Protestant, I had no idea of what he was talking about nor did I understand the significance of this event. In the churches I had attended, very little was discussed about Mary, except at Christmas time. We, of course, knew she was with Jesus throughout his ministry and that she had stayed with Him until the end of his death on the cross, even when others close to Him had fled. That was pretty much the extent of what I had been taught about the Virgin Mary. I don't recall hearing any stories about the role she played in the growth of the Church after Pentecost. I was quite certain that I had never heard anything about her assumption into heaven. I was not at ease with this thought and my "Catholic suspicions" began to stir up inside me. I wanted to check with Judy to see how she was feeling about this but decided I'd keep this to myself for the time being.

While keeping an open mind about this was difficult for me, the idea that women had played an important role in the early church was not. I had no problem accepting that their role was probably more important than the credit they had been given. Even today, I don't think a single church could survive without the support of the female members. The women at the church I grew up in were always the first ones on the scene to help in times of trouble. Almost all of my Sunday School teachers had been women. I knew it was Mary who had pushed Jesus to perform His first public miracle, at a wedding. Jesus did not think it was yet His time. His Mother evidently thought it was, but still left this up to Him. It was the "other" Mary who found the angels at the empty tomb. She is the one that brought the first word to the disciples that Jesus was not in His tomb. Still, this whole idea of Mary's Assumption and a Feast Day was going to require some additional explaining to me. I also needed to understand why certain dates were referred to as feast days and others were referred to as fast days. The Catholics seemed to have so many unfamiliar traditions that were challenging to me simply because I had never heard of them. All of these things continued to stir up my suspicions. The Catholics in our group seemed to take it for granted that everyone knew all about these things. They really didn't seem to understand just how big of a jump all of this actually was for a Protestant. It became very obvious that both Catholics and Protestants were very sequestered from each other's traditions. While we might have some idea of what our differences were, we had no actual understanding of those differences. I began to wonder if the different denominations simply criticized each other on a lot of misinformation or limited knowledge. Maybe the Protestants had missed how important Mary was to the church or maybe the Catholics were trying to elevate her to a more prominent role. If that were true, that would, however, lead to the question, "Why? Why would elevating her be important?" I didn't have the answers, so I dismissed the thought and began taking in the town again through my bus window.

Medjugorje was small! It was much smaller than I had expected and I immediately began to look for the hotels and restaurants that would house and feed all the people piling into town. It didn't take our tour bus long, even at a slow pace, to make it through to the other side of the village. Looking out the window I didn't see a single hotel and only one small restaurant. I couldn't imagine how this village was going to take care of all these people and thought this, in and of itself, would be one of the miracles here. It looked to me like we would be in need of a modern day "loaves and fishes" blessing. The bus made its way through part of the village toward our final stop.

I had no idea what kind of accommodations we would be staying in. I didn't know if we would be staying at an individual's house or some other kind of facility. It was not like me to go anywhere without firming up these kinds of details, so I turned again to Judy and asked her if she knew where we would be staying. Judy wasn't sure either, but this didn't seem to bother her in the least. All she knew was that we would be staying with a family. I remembered someone had told me that many of the local families would give up their beds and sleep on the floor to make room for those who traveled to Medjugorje. This was a practice that had started in the early days, when the first pilgrims began coming. We were told this was done out of a sense of charity toward the pilgrims. I was hoping that no one would be sleeping on the floor to accommodate us. I knew this would make me very uncomfortable and I wondered how it would make them feel if we were to refuse.

The bus came to a full stop and I was hoping this meant we were finally at our destination. I glanced at my watch and it was just shy of being twenty-two hours since we had departed Jacksonville. My bottom end felt numb and was proof of this fact. As I looked out the window, I saw two young adults and a child standing beside the road. When the bus doors opened, Dragan rushed out to greet the young couple and it was obvious they were not strangers. I thought they appeared to be too young to be our host family but from the way they were talking and smiling I realized I was wrong. The bus was parked outside of a four story fairly modern structure. From the outside, it appeared to be fairly new and, fortunately, it was large enough for everyone in

our group to stay here. I later found out that many new resi-
dent homes like this had been built specifically to house
the pilgrims. I affectionately began referring to these multi-
bedroom homes as "Pilgrim's Inns."

In just a few moments, Dragan re-entered the bus
and announced that this was, in fact, the home where we
would be staying. Everyone quickly gathered their belongings, eager to get off the bus and view our new home for
the next five days. As we stepped off the bus one by one,
our new host appeared to be very happy to see us. I was
beat and all I wanted was to get our room key and find our
room! Fortunately, unloading the bus was a quick and easy
process since we had lost our luggage and there was very
little to take off, other than the few small carry-on bags.
Stepping out of the air-conditioned bus, I was immediately
hit with the afternoon heat. It was now Saturday afternoon
in Medjugorje and the temperature had to be at least a 100
degrees and very dry. I was happy to find that it was not
going to be as humid as the Florida we had left behind. I
thought the heat, minus the humidity, would make it a lot
easier for all of us to deal with.

JUDY

*I was as excited as everyone else to get off the bus. We
walked into the dining area and Dragan announced that this*

would be our main meeting area during the week. Don and I were assigned our room on the second floor. There were no elevators and so we eagerly climbed the stairs to find our corner room. There were no keys assigned to any of us and, interestingly enough, no one seemed to be bothered by this. In fact, for some reason it seemed perfectly normal, considering we were all staying in someone's home. When we opened the door to our room, we found it spotless but very starkly furnished. There was a dresser, a bed and a small Crucifix that hung on the wall over the bed. I walked into the room ahead of Don and opened a door which I thought was going to be the closet. I was pleasantly surprised, to say the least, to find that we had our very own bathroom. As Don made his way into the room and placed our carry-on bags on the dresser, he immediately turned to me shaking his head and pointed to the bed. I could not help but laugh. Don is 6 ft. 3 and the bed looked like it was made for one of Snow White's seven dwarfs. It would not have been so much of a problem except for the fact that it had an elevated foot board that extended high above the top of the mattress. There was no way Don was going to fit on that bed. We quickly decided the two of us could take the bed apart and put the mattress on the floor. This didn't take us but a couple of minutes to accomplish and Don placed the head and foot boards in the corner of the room. We both dropped down on the mattress to test it out.

Next to the bed was a slim, but tall, casement window and Don decided to open it to create some cross ventilation by leaving the door ajar. He wasn't at all happy to find that there was no screen in the window. We had all been warned about the mosquitoes and we had been told how important it was to bring repellant. Lucky for us, we had packed ours in our carry-on bags. Even though there was no air conditioning, the ceiling height was at least ten feet high, so between the fan, the open window and the cracked door, we thought we would manage pretty well. As I looked out our window, I realized we had a perfect view of the large cross on Mt. Krizevac. Terri had told us about the huge cross that had been erected by the villagers on the top of this mountain. There it was directly in front of us. From our second floor window, it looked like you could probably see this cross from almost any place in the village. I knew this was the mountain on which I had seen all those feet climbing up in my dream three months earlier. I couldn't believe I was finally here. Looking at the mountain, I contemplated the fact that it had already been quite a journey just to get here, and yet we were really just beginning it. I also knew from Terri that, locally, this mountain called Mount Krizevac, would simply become know to us and all pilgrims as Cross Mountain. There was another significant hill near the village that was known as Podboro and I looked around wondering if I could see that from our window

too. Podboro was the hill where the Virgin Mary had report-
edly first appeared to the six children. It was here that they
had initially run away in fear but had later returned to see
her beckoning them to come closer. From our vantage point,
Podboro was not visible.

As we began to settle in, we heard someone from the group
calling everyone back down to a meeting. Don thought about
skipping the meeting to rest but I grabbed his hand, pulled
him off the bed and convinced him we should go. Everyone
in our group was gathered in the dining room and we could
hear brief discussions about what items had arrived and who
had soap or toothpaste. Some of the older people in our group
were unhappy that there was no elevator and their room
was on the top floor. Several of the younger people who had
ended up with rooms on the lower level quickly volunteered
to exchange rooms with them. This began a series of trading
and sharing items, including our clothes. Everyone was run-
ning in and out of each other's rooms to accommodate each
other's needs. We had no idea of when, or even if, our luggage
would arrive before we were to leave.

Traveling with our group was a young priest from the
Diocese of Pensacola-Tallahassee by the name of Father
Mike Cherup and he dutifully reminded us that we needed to
give thanks for our safe travel. As he gave thanks, he prayed
that God would grant to each of us a deeper understanding

of His love during our stay in Medjugorje. When the prayer was over, our guide began to give us a lengthy orientation of Medjugorje, its events and the lay of the land. After hearing this, I wasn't worried that we would easily get lost. There was Mt. Krizevac, (known as Cross Mountain), Mount Podboro, (known as Apparition Hill), St. James Church and the main road where there were a couple of restaurants and gifts shops. That was pretty much it, other than the homes of several of the visionaries. Some of the daily events were laid out for us as well. The apparitions took place at 6:40 p.m. each evening at St. James Church. During the day, there would be several meetings for Mass carried on in the different languages of the many pilgrims that were present. Today, the English Mass would be at 5 p.m. and it would be over in time for the daily Rosary. Dragan explained that The Rosary is prayed every day just before the apparition and that confessions would also be available during the day. Our first group event, tomorrow morning, would be a walk up Cross Mountain. We would be awakened at 4:30 and leave at 5:30 a.m. Don moaned and whispered to me, "You gotta be kidding." We had been traveling for twenty-two hours and we had also lost six hours due to the time difference. All of this had begun to work on us. We were told that leaving this early would be best because we would miss the crowds and also the heat of the day. Many moaned but everyone accepted this.

We had barely caught our breath before things starting happening. We were advised we would have just enough time to make it to the English Mass if we left immediately. After Mass, we could attend the Rosary outside the church and then an apparition at 6:40 p.m. Dinner would be served in our dining room when we returned. Everyone quickly scrambled out the door and we began walking the two short blocks towards St. James for Mass.

DON

The road to the church was hard packed dirt and quite dusty. Only the main road coming in to Medjugorje was paved at the time and it looked as if it had only been paved a short time before we arrived. Prior to the apparitions, Medjugorje was so insignificant you could not find it on any map of Yugoslavia. As we walked to the church, I noticed my back was not hurting. In fact, it had not bothered me at all during the long flight or the three hour bus drive in. That, in itself, was pretty surprising to me. Just three weeks before we had left, I was flat on my back with a pinched disc in my lower back and I had not been able to turn over while lying down without Judy's help. I had been very concerned it might erupt again on the trip and this had added to my other anxieties about coming. For this reason alone, I had wondered if I would be able to make the trip. Others had physical concerns as well, including Page from Judy's office, who was five months pregnant. I thought about what Bob had told me, regarding the stories he had heard about others traveling to Medjugorje who had many apprehensions and physical problems. Once they had gotten on the plane, he said, their ailments had disappeared. I was pretty amazed that my back actually felt like nothing had ever been wrong with it.

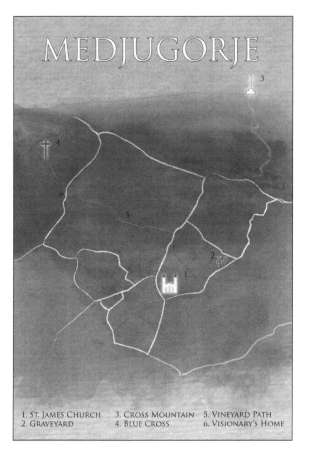

Map of Medjugorje

As we walked the short distance towards the church, I began to take in the town, as it related to Dragan's orientation of Medjugorje. {See Medjugorje Map} Medjugorje sat on a plain surrounded in the east by Apparition Hill, which was about three hundred feet high. The site of the first apparition was marked on the hill by a simple wooden cross that everyone called the "Blue Cross." We later learned that blue is the color most often associated with the Virgin. About 1,700 feet high and overshadowing the plains to the southwest, towered Cross Mountain. St. James Church was located to the west of Apparition Hill and to the north of Cross Mountain. The central location of St. James made an almost perfect triangle between these three significant landmarks. Along the path up Cross Mountain, the villagers had erected round bronze monuments in 1988, depicting the events leading up to Christ's death on the Cross.

In just a few minutes, we were in front of The Church of St. James, with its two clock towers on each side of the main entrance. The church was surrounded by fields and vineyards and Cross Mountain was a backdrop just a mile or so behind the church. We quickly learned that St. James was the central place of prayer for the thousands of pilgrims who came to Medjugorje, as well as for the local villagers. At 6:40 p.m., The Virgin was to appear to the visionaries in the east tower and I was eager to be there to witness this. Perhaps we would see the visionaries as they made their way into the church. I didn't know how I would react or even what to expect, but this was no doubt one of the main reasons all these people were here. I had come a long way to be near this and I did not plan on missing it either.

St. James Church with Cross Mountain in the left background

As we approached the front of the church yard, it was quite congested. An earlier Mass had just ended and there was a steady flow of people leaving that Mass by passing others who were going in for the next. There were hundreds of people just standing in the courtyard and many were milling around a statue of the Virgin Mary, called "Queen of Peace." This statue was made of white marble and held a prominent place in the front courtyard of the church. The figure of Mary was just slightly larger than human size and it was encircled by a brick wall about two feet high, with a short steel picket fence on top of the wall. The wall formed a perfect circle around the statue and rose bushes had been planted inside the fenced area. This beautiful statue of Mary was one of the first things to catch my eye on the way to the front doors of the church. The next thing that caught my attention was all of the notes and sealed envelopes tied to the pickets of the fence. Terri pointed these out to us as we walked by. She explained that they contain the prayers that had been left behind during the day. Each day, the notes and envelopes were gathered and presented to the Virgin, at the time of the apparition. Writing down prayers was a foreign idea to me and I decided it was just another one of those "Catholic" things. In a few minutes the Catholic Mass would begin and I had a feeling that I was about to witness, yet another, unfamiliar practice.

Statue of The Queen of Peace of Medjugorje

Approaching the church, I had noticed the simple beauty of St. James. The church had a stone courtyard in the front and it was surrounded on the other sides by gravel. Just a few minutes before we entered the church, Terri pointed out the window on the west side of the church, where the Virgin Mary had appeared to her, Mary and Karen. The bench she had talked about was still there, directly under the window, and I wondered if anyone else had stood on that bench and witnessed what they had. As we walked through the massive doorway of St. James and into the main sanctuary of the chapel I again noticed the simplicity of the church. The floors were stone and the pews were plain wood benches. There was a total absence of the refinements of plush carpet, cushioned pews and ornate trim that I was accustomed to in the churches I had attended back home in the United States. The original church had been built in 1897 on grounds that were subject to earthquakes. The old church had begun to sink and was leaning badly, so in the early 1930's plans were drawn up for a new church to be built. The construction of St. James took over thirty-five years to complete, beginning in 1934 and finishing in January of 1969. The size of St. James seemed much more suited for a large town rather than a tiny parish the size of Medjugorje. When the church was first being built, many of the villagers had complained that the church was too large and too expensive. This would become one of those coincidental things that later proved to be of great significance; forty seven years later this parish church found itself responsible for meeting the needs of thousands of people who would be traveling here each and every week. As we took our seats near the middle of the church, I began to watch the church filling up and then overflowing its capacity. While waiting for Mass to begin, I marveled at the connection of all the events leading up to the beginning of the Apparition.

This was my first Catholic Mass and I had no idea of what I was supposed to do during it. Earlier, I had felt certain they would provide a program outlining the service for us, but I was wrong. I knew there was going to be a lot of standing, kneeling and sitting down, but I didn't have a clue when I was supposed to do it. I decided I would just follow the people in front of me and hope they were Catholic and familiar with the service. The service began with the hymn, "The Battle Hymn of the Republic." I could hardly believe I was hearing this familiar hymn that had been written during the American Civil War, here, in such a faraway land. It was an English Mass but still it astonished me and I looked at Judy and smiled at the surprise. I noticed many people were raising their hands in worship, which reminded me more of the Pentecostal services I had witnessed a few times in my youth. For some reason, I had not expected that during a Catholic Mass. The two Lutherans in our group definitely had an advantage over the two Baptists when it came to following the order of a liturgical service. We managed to follow all the ups and downs, with only a few seconds of lag time. Most of the priests presiding over the Mass appeared to be from England, Ireland or the United States, from the sounds of their voices. Their message soon was to become a familiar message to pray, fast, confess, read the Bible and revere the Eucharist. After hearing the familiar songs and the English-speaking priest, I began to feel more at ease and, perhaps, a little less out of place.

Toward the end of the Mass, the priest began preparing for the Holy Eucharist. Many Franciscan priests moved throughout the crowd, offering the bread and then the wine. I was used to this being referred to as "The Lord's Supper," in our Baptist Church. There, we used tiny saltine crackers and grape juice. There was something about how this was presided over, and also dispersed, that made the ceremony seem more meaningful and very holy. In the Baptist Church, any baptized believer could partake and we were not yet aware that, in the Catholic Church, the Eucharist was not extended to non-Catholics. There were no questions asked or warning given prior to going to Mass, so Judy and I, as well as the other Protestants in our group, eagerly participated. Our traveling priest and spiritual advisor, Father Mike, had later asked others in our group to make us aware of this. When we first heard that we should not participate in communion it seemed very non-inclusive and something that separated us from each other. We didn't understand or feel this was right but, in the end, we decided we should respect the rules of the Catholic Church.

When Mass was over, our exit from the church was much slower than our entrance. As we made our way out into the courtyard, we were enveloped by an even greater throng of people. Many were pushing their way to the front of the church as we were moving out away from the front of the church. Once we made it outside, there was a definite energy in the air. A crowd was gathering just outside the east clock tower and you could see a window was open. Conversations were all centered on the impending apparition while we waited for someone to begin the Rosary. Judy and I had each been given a Rosary now, so this would be our first attempt at actually participating in this prayer.

Waiting for the Rosary to begin gave me an excellent opportunity to eavesdrop on conversations from the crowd. I learned that the apparition would take place in the east tower, in the room where I could see the open window. Someone would close the window when the apparition began, allowing people outside to know when to become silent. Once the apparition was over, they would then re-open the window. I felt sort of strange, just standing there waiting for a window to open and close. I wondered, "Is this all we're going to witness? Did we come thousands of miles just to look up to see a window open and close? How could this be enough to bring all these people here?" My thoughts were interrupted when someone began to lead the group in praying the Rosary. It seemed like we were about halfway through the prayer when an unexpected wind came through and birds, which I had not heard before, began chirping loudly. Goose-bumps involuntarily ran up my arms. I wondered where all these birds had come from and realized that they must have been roosting in the trees, scattered here and there around the courtyard. Simultaneously, everyone stopped praying and I heard someone from behind us whisper, "She is here!" Looking up at the tower I saw the window close. I was not sure what had happened, but it felt like something more physical than spiritual. I heard another person whisper to someone nearby, "She always comes on a wind and just before she appears, the birds sing her coming." More goose-bumps ran up my arm and I thought, "My God, could this really be happening here?" I was in awe at the possibility that I could be standing just a few feet away from the Mother of Jesus. How do you begin to accept the possibility of this? The idea of her appearing here, just a few feet from me, was incredible, wonderful, and certainly mysterious, but at the same time, it was a little disturbing. I was taken by a sudden moment of guilt with a mixture of true humility. I had fought coming so much. It was starting to sink in that I had almost missed being here. Even though I could not comprehend an apparition, I found myself wanting to know and to understand what was going on behind those walls in the tower. I did not ask the question again: "Was I here just to see a window open and close?"

I knew that coming to Medjugorje was a spiritual journey for many, but I had felt something physical: the wind, the birds and the involuntary rush that ran through my body.

While the window was closed, the crowd was in complete silence. The window remained closed for about twenty minutes and then it reopened and the crowd erupted in applause, which I thought was an unusual response. I think it was simply a spontaneous expression of excitement and joy. In just a few minutes, everyone began praying the Rosary again from the place we had left off before. When the Rosary was over, the crowd began to break up. I turned to Judy and just raised my eyebrows, not really knowing what to say. Our communication, by expression, seemed to be met by mutual agreement. I felt like I should say something, but what? Judy couldn't seem to come up with any words either.

Waiting with the crowd outside the apparition window

It was still light out but the sun was now low in the sky. A good portion of the crowd appeared to be headed to the back of the church, I assumed, to look at the sun set. This small and quaint little hamlet seemed much more alive now. We were still standing there, on the east side of the church, and I gazed up at the cross on Cross Mountain. It captured my gaze for several minutes, as my thoughts drifted to the walk we were going to take up there the next morning. Terri was standing nearby and heard me ask, "Well, what's next?" "Dinner, I think," was her reply, as she looked at me smiling. I just knew she wanted to know what I was thinking. You could see she was excited for us and I could sense she was looking for some affirmation that I was as excited or perhaps moved as she was. I reached over and gave her a hug and said, "Let's go eat!" Although I felt a renewed energy and anticipation, I was still not ready to share any of my thoughts. All of this was going to require some thinking and reflection first.

Dinner was so much better than I had expected. The aroma of hot food and the fellowship began to capture everyone. Our meal consisted of delicious fresh vegetables, including the best tomatoes I had ever tasted in my life, along with meat and great European bread (hard on the outside and soft in the middle). I was extremely tired but found myself feeling very relaxed and getting comfortable with my surroundings. The buzz around the table was naturally about the apparition. People were expressing their thoughts and their questions: "What did she say? How did you feel? Did you notice the birds sing and the wind come up?" We were disappointed that none of us had witnessed the visionaries enter the church this day. Everyone would have to wait until the following day to find out what message had been given during the apparition. We were told the visionaries, or "Seers" as they were also called, would write down the message and someone would later post it at the church.

JUDY

As soon as dinner was over, the discussion turned to what everyone was planning to do with the rest of the evening. Some were interested only in getting to bed early, knowing that we would be getting up at 4:30 a.m. to climb Cross Mountain. Several in our group wanted to find their way over to Apparition Hill, where the Blue Cross had been erected, at the spot of the first apparition. Despite the fact that we had little rest in over twenty-six hours, Don and I had gotten our second wind and we eagerly joined in for this trek. I had no idea where we were going in the dark but someone seemed to know the way. The path over was a little off the main road and we walked through vineyards and came to a group of several small homes near the base of the hill. It appeared everyone here went to bed early because there were no noises coming from any of the houses.

Don seemed to be going with the flow a lot easier now and I was very relieved and happy to see it.

The walk didn't take us that long and once we got to the base of Mt. Podboro, or Apparition Hill, we walked up just a short distance more. The hill was extremely rocky and we had to weave our way through the rocks and thorn bushes. The thorns on these bushes were easily three inches long and I realized that stumbling or falling against one of these would be very painful. Eventually, we made our way through the night without encountering a mishap, and found our way to the small "Blue Cross."

The night was incredibly clear and, despite the large number of people below in the village, it was amazingly quiet. There was no traffic noise and the night was finally beginning to cool down. It looked like someone had moved several of the larger rocks or small boulders around so people could sit on them in front of this simple small blue cross. Without instruction, each person seemed to be drawn to one of these rocks and everyone sat quietly with their own thoughts. The setting was remarkable and, for some reason, it reminded me of the biblical pictures I had seen of Jesus when He was praying in the Garden of Gethsemane. There were the large rocks, the thick shrubs that formed a privacy wall around us, and the small village below, with the few lights flickering. We were all there together, *praying silently to ourselves, as naturally as sheep drawn to water at the end of a hot day.*

There was no moon this night and it was one of the clearest nights I had ever seen. There were so many brilliant stars completely covering the sky. I love being outside in nature, and this was a perfect night to be here to enjoy this peaceful setting and the beautiful night sky. After a while, another small group quietly intruded upon us and asked if it would be O.K. if they joined us. We didn't mind. We were all there for the same reason- to be quiet and feel God's presence. Someone in their group had also brought a guitar and, at some point, he picked it up and began to play quietly. The songs were simple and soon we all joined in singing songs of praise. As we were singing, a huge shooting star streaked across the sky. Many of us were gazing up at the beautiful star filled sky and almost everyone saw it. In a few minutes, there was another and suddenly they were coming so fast we could hardly count them. I had never witnessed anything like it and I wondered if it was another phenomenon of this special place. They were coming so close together and blazing from one side of the sky to the other. We later learned that we had been given a front seat to the annual Perseids Meteor Shower that occurs each August. It was an amazing spectacle to witness in such a beautiful setting. How wonderful, I thought, that we would be here at this

time, outside looking up at the sky. It felt like God's fireworks,
celebrating our arrival in Medjugorje.

Another group we met at the Blue Cross turned the night into

song

Judy (second from the left) with others at the base
of the Blue Cross on our first evening where we witnessed the Perseids meteor shower

**The heavens declare the glory of God;
the sky proclaims its builder's craft.**

**Psalms 19:1
The New American Bible**

Chapter 9

A Mountain to Climb

JUDY

*I*t felt like we had been asleep for only two or three hours when I heard people talking and walking down the concrete hall just outside our door. I heard Don moan under his breath as he rolled off the mattress and onto the floor. I wasn't at all ready to get up and tried to push all the noise out of my mind and go back to sleep. Don started pushing on me and telling me it was time to get up. I rolled over, just looked at him and he responded with, "I know." I am the hard sleeper in our family, so when he said he would take a shower first I was more than happy to let him go, so I could sleep a few more minutes. As I tried to go back to sleep, I could hear Don talking in the bathroom. Something about violations of building codes and steel protruding out from the walls that were too small and the one-necked light bulb that* *was hanging down from the ceiling. I groaned and pulled the pillow over my head. This was something I had grown used to, as the wife of a building contractor. Don had an eye for good craftsmanship and beautiful architecture. He also had a keen eye for poor craftsmanship. We never went anywhere that he didn't inspect the buildings. If I ever found a house I really liked, he would tear it apart, pointing out the flaws. It used to make me crazy. I'd find a beautiful home for sale, something I thought would be perfect for us and I didn't care if they used the wrong size nails on the deck or the joist didn't fit right. I didn't even know what a joist was.*

I heard Don finally turn on the shower and I heard him yell..."Awhhhh...the shower is great," so I began to stir and woke myself up, anticipating a nice, warm shower to get me going. Don soon turned off the shower came out of the small bathroom and told me we only had a few more minutes and that I needed to hurry if I wanted any breakfast. I quickly jumped in, expecting a nice shower, and no sooner than I had soap all over me, the water turned ice cold. I yelled out to Don, "There is no more hot water."

He answered back, "I was afraid that might happen. I think they use solar heat." I was not a happy camper, rinsing off in ice cold water, but I quickly learned that getting up first was going to be important this week. As bad as this early morning experience was, I had to admit it woke me up and I felt totally invigorated and now fully ready for the new day.

Everyone was gathering in the dining room and we all rushed through our breakfast to get on our way as soon as possible. It was going to take us about five hours to make the trip up Cross Mountain and back. Although this was incredibly early, we were all glad to beat the heat. As our group began walking through the village, the sun was just beginning to rise over Apparition Hill and there was a light early morning fog. Everyone still seemed a little quieter and less conversational than usual this morning, probably because it was so early. We could hear roosters crowing off and on from different directions throughout the village, reminding us of our rural setting. Other reminders of the local economy and how people here made their living were found in the pungent smells of the farming community's cows, horses and chickens that were in the family pens we passed. There were also sun tobacco fields and vineyards and small flocks of sheep getting ready to be sheared. On our way, we began to pass several families making their way towards the village, most likely to open up their shops or attend morning Mass. One family looked similar to the next and the men and women seemed to have one type of basic wardrobe. Most of the men wore a traditional black hat, a white shirt with a black vest under a black coat and black shoes or work boots. The women wore long black or dark colored dresses or skirts. Most of the older women wore a scarf on their head. As they passed us, they were so warm and friendly and always smiled and nodded hello. It was refreshing to see older brothers carrying their younger siblings on their shoulders as they all walked together as a family unit into the village. It was like being on a movie set with characters dressed up in costumes to depict people from centuries gone by in Poland or, yes, I guess even Yugoslavia. Only it was 1990 and these people were real and alive today. It was so hard to imagine a place so unspoiled like this still existed. We had little in common with these rural people in the former Yugoslavia, but there was something so attractive about their simple life. As we got closer to the base of Cross Mountain, we turned up a hilly road and found a few little shops there. I assumed they were there as a last stop for water or Rosaries before the long ascension up the mountain. From this vantage point, climbers could look down on the village and see all the roof tops, vineyard and fields. In the distance, the twin towers of Saint James could be seen, breaking through the fog and rising high above everything else in the village. It was a beautiful sight, especially this early in the morning.

Villagers walking into Medjugorje as we are on our way toward Cross Mountain early in the morning

Before we began our climb, Fr. Mike gathered us and gave us a pamphlet that had all the prayers we would be praying at each of the "Stations of the Cross," which was also called "The Way of the Cross," by some in our group. I was not at all familiar with this prayer or practice and, realizing there were those in the group that were not Catholic, Fr. Mike began to explain it to us. On our path up Cross Mountain there would be fifteen places, or "stations", where the bronze, circular monuments would be. Each monument would have a scene etched on it, reminding us of a particular event that Christ had gone through during His final hours before He was crucified. We would stop at each "station" for prayer *and meditate upon each of the scenes of Christ's suffering and death on the cross. The first station would be Jesus praying in the Garden of Gethsemane, the night before He was arrested; the next would be when **Pilate** condemned Him to death; the next depicted when they placed the cross on His shoulder, and on we would continue in His steps, until His death on the cross and finally when Jesus was being placed in His tomb. A fifteenth station had also been added beneath the Cross, showing the Resurrection of Christ. The final stop would be on top of the mountain, where we would finally be at the base of the huge 30-foot high cross we had all seen from such a long distance the moment we arrived in Medjugorje. While I had never prayed the "Stations of the Cross" before, suddenly all these things that seemed liked strange Catholic traditions became quite beautiful to me.*

I was very familiar with the story of what happened to Jesus, between his arrest and Crucifixion, but I had never taken so much time before to really think or meditate on what He had gone through. Why would I? Who wanted to think about anyone's suffering? I knew the story had a happy ending; so, true to my personality, that's more of what I thought we should focus on. Even still, somehow, here on this mountain I was beginning to understand the importance of remembering His suffering. Meditating on how much He had suffered was a way of remembering, and, more importantly, understanding how much He truly loved us.

DON

After hearing Fr. Mike's explanation of 'the Stations of the Cross,' we began our trip up the mountain. It was beginning to appear that there was a prayer for every event on this trip. I was quite certain I had never prayed this much before; not even when my Florida State Football team was behind with three minutes left in the game or when I was on an extremely turbulent flight had I prayed this much. It seemed these Catholics had a formal prayer for everything. We had a morning prayer, then a blessing for our food and now a prayer for our climb up the mountain, and then at least fifteen more prayers would be prayed on the way up the mountain before we reached the top. There was nothing said about a prayer at the top of the mountain, but I imagined there would be one for that too. I was certain by the end of this week I would be caught up on my prayers for at least a year. As we made our way to the first station, Fr. Mike led us in prayer. I noticed there were a number of shoes left here and I couldn't imagine why anyone would want to make their way up this rough path barefoot. I later learned that people did this as a way to further identify with Christ's suffering. I had not yet caught on to the significance of participating in Christ's suffering. I could see the sharp rocks protruding from the trail and I quickly decided this was not for me. As we continued on up the mountain to the next station, we could hear people praying the Rosary in many different languages. There was a certain cadence to this prayer so, no matter what the language, we knew what we were hearing.

Bronze monoliths depict the Stations of the Cross where pilgrims leave their prayer petitions. The wooden cross to the left was the original Station of the Cross before the newer monoliths were installed.

The path up Cross Mountain was not what I would really call a path. I could see where I was to go, but it was not a well defined path. It was basically made up of large broken rocks resembling our Florida limestone, only these were much harder. Most were sharp rocks that protruded out of the ground. Some were set firm in the earth, but others were loose and would move when you stepped on them wrong. There were lots of places to slip or stub your toes and the rocks could easily cut into the soles of your shoes. I still could not believe anyone would choose to walk this path barefooted. By the time I had gotten to the fourth station, my feet were killing me.

The treacherous rocky path up Cross Mountain.

I was beginning to get really perturbed, thinking about the airline's failure to get my luggage, with my hiking boots, on the plane. All I had now were these very thin, soft soled deck shoes. With each additional step, I began to fear I would slip and twist my ankle, or worse, throw out my back. Even though my back had been feeling fine, I still thought about what would happen if my back went out on this mountain. I could imagine how hard it would be to get me back down. Something told me there were no chiropractors anywhere near Medjugorje and the thought of having that kind of pain, with no doctor, was not anything I wanted to experience while here. It was hard to concentrate on the prayers when I was mumbling obscenities at these rocks and cursing the airlines for leaving my rock climbing boots behind.

At one point, I paused to look back and take in the beauty of the valley and the fields below and, suddenly, I realized I was ignoring my surroundings, worrying about my feet and my back. I was so immersed in my thoughts I had not noticed the people above me had moved off to the side to allow a group of older villagers some space to move by us on their way down. I reached to grab hold of a boulder, to balance myself, and that's when I saw a group of elderly women, who appeared to be in their eighty's, pass me by barefooted. As they passed us, they were all smiling and I could hear their prayers resume as they trailed off on down the path. I felt completely ashamed and quite humbled by this sight. These simple, elderly women were teaching me something. Here I was, a large 6'3" man in his early forties, mumbling about my feet hurting. These women were old enough to be my grandmother and they weren't complaining. Instead, they were taking joy in this journey of prayer. It was just what I needed to witness to help me refocus and turn my attention back to the prayers and what they represented. I decided I needed to stop worrying about my feet and my back.

By now, we were at another station and it was a nice place to stop and look back around. We were slowly but surely moving on up the mountain and the view was becoming increasingly spectacular. Gazing back on St. James, in the valley surrounded by vineyards and farm land, it struck me how much this looked like an ancient biblical scene. Jesus had taught in parables using much of His surroundings, just like the sheep, the wheat and the vineyard we passed on our way up. He also spoke about the faith to move mountains. All of that was here and this place somehow set an inspiring stage for the events we were beginning to witness first hand. It was impossible to escape all the similarities. "God, what a setting!" I mumbled out loud. Judy was right behind me and I knew she must have heard me. I turned around to look at her and she greeted me with a big smile of agreement as we joined in the prayer at the station where Simon of Cyrene stopped to help Jesus carry His cross. We prayed that we, too, would join in to help Jesus when needed.

The thought of God hearing Judy's prayer and inviting her to come here and share all of this was really beginning to sink in. I listened more intently to Fr. Mike, and his words were not escaping me now. True, it had been Judy who had been invited and I was just along for the ride, but I remembered what the lady said somewhere in the Bible, "Yes, Lord, but even the dogs get to eat the crumbs from the Master's table." I wasn't sure, but I was beginning to feel like somehow, I was getting more than just a portion of the crumbs. It felt like I was beginning to receive something here on Cross Mountain. The setting, it's path, the meditations on the suffering of Christ, as well as the large cross on top of this mountain, were all beginning to speak to me. I was not missing the symbolism of it all. The climb to the top of the mountain was turning into something more than an adventure to get to the top or to see a magnificent cross or to get a breathtaking view. Our climb was beginning to tell me something about my life.

Just moments ago I had been complaining about my feet and worrying about my back. I was perturbed at the airlines for not having my boots to help me on my walk up the mountain. I had already been brought out of my complaining about my feet by the cheerful women walking by with bare feet. Now I found myself stopping to pray in front of a scene where Christ suffering was shared by a common man, Simon, who had not expected that his journey to town would end in the sharing of Christ's burden by helping carrying his cross. Like Simon, I came to this mountain not expecting anything. I also found myself unexpectedly drawn in to an understanding of what Christ had to endure on his way to the cross. I remember beginning to feel a real heaviness in my heart, and maybe a little shame, as I turned back to the path and continued on.

By now, the slope had begun to get increasingly steeper and steeper. At one point, it seemed like we were literally climbing rocks. In some places, we would have to grab rocks ahead of us and steady ourselves, as we used the rocks to pull us forward. At each station, I could not help but to think more and more about Christ and the uniqueness of this trail. It was a lot like my own walk with God. Sometimes it wasn't clear where I was going or where my life was heading. I could just keep walking, trying to make the right steps, but there was always a chance I could slip and fall on a sharp rock or run into one of these three inch thorns if I wasn't careful. The symbolism of this path was clear to me. If I kept going, took time to rest along the way, kept my mind and heart on the things of God (and not my feet), ultimately I would find my way. It seemed like if the path was easy and didn't cost me anything, I was willing to go along; however, if it started to get too uncomfortable or I wasn't sure where the path was leading, I could just as easily find something else to think about. To tell you the truth, I could always find something to distract me from getting too close. I seem to have a spirit of resistance in me that kept me from getting too close to anything, especially God. I don't believe I had ever truly surrendered. I did want to once. Once, I did have a real calling to surrender, back that time Billy Graham came to Tallahassee. But after what happened there I would never let my guard down again. It was very troubling and painful for me to think about that, so I chose not to. Being here in this setting, however, was stirring up all those feelings for me again. Here I was now, climbing a mountain in Yugoslavia and beginning to feel comfortable with being here. I wasn't going to let that painful, secret memory interfere with what I felt here, so I pushed it as far out of my mind as I possibly could and again turned back to my surroundings.

I looked down the trail and saw Terri and her mother. They had stopped to rest and her mother, Barbara, had found a large stone to sit on. Terri was kneeling in front of her on the trail. There was a beautiful look of love and closeness on their faces, as they talked quietly by themselves. It made me think of my own mother and for some reason I was remembering her singing at church in her high pitched, off tune voice: "I surrender, I surrender all." I don't remember the rest of that song, but I can remember how she would just belt it out with so much joy, not worrying if she was in tune or not. I have seen so many people here with that kind of joy. People seemed so comfortable lifting their hands in worship and praise. I was keenly aware that, even though I was getting more comfortable in this place, I was not close to feeling that kind of joy - not even here.

As we continued up the mountain and prayed at the last Station of the Cross, we all made our way, one by one, to the top of the mountain. We were finally standing beneath the large stone cross, free to wander about on our own. As a contractor, I marveled at the monumental task it must have been to have moved all the materials up this same path to erect the cross. They used no machinery, just sheer brawn and a belief that God would reward this village for their faith. Based on everything that was going on here now, fifty-six years after the cross had been erected, it seemed God had indeed looked favorably upon this tiny village and was using it to bring people from all over the world closer to Him.

The cross dominated the mountain and I tried to imagine what it must have been like for a small community of people to make such a mighty decision to build this cross way up here. I wondered what had motivated them. Later in the day, I would learn that Pope Pius XI, had shared a dream that he had earlier, in 1933, about a cross being raised on the highest hill in Herzegovina. The parish priest in Medjugorje at the time heard about this dream and shared it with the people of his parish. They immediately decided to take on the task of erecting the cross here. When word of their actions got back to Pope Pius XI, he had been very moved and decided to send the parish a gift. The gift he sent was a part of a relic that was taken from the cross believed to be the true Cross of Jesus; it came from the Church of the Holy Cross, in Jerusalem. The relic was then built into the intersection of the arms of this magnificent cross. Understanding how difficult it was to erect the cross on such a high mountain, I realized what a statement they were making. They were acknowledging Jesus Christ as their Savior and Lord and proclaiming it to the world by this cross. They were saying it is in Him that we place our trust and our future. What courage they displayed by taking such a faithful stand to build a thirty foot tall, sixteen ton concrete cross on the top of the highest mountain in Bosnia, Herzegovina during pre-

World War II, with the Nazi empire growing and Fascist regimes springing up in this part of the world.

As I got closer to the cross, I saw an inscription the villagers had placed on the cross. In a moment someone was translating the inscription to me...

"TO JESUS CHRIST, THE REDEEMER OF THE HUMAN RACE, AS A SIGN OF OUR FAITH, LOVE AND HOPE, IN REMEMBRANCE OF THE 1900TH ANNIVERSARY OF THE PASSION OF JESUS"

I had heard sermons about "faith without action." There should be no question as to their faith, by the actions they put behind this proclamation. It was a major undertaking, not to mention a courageous act to make a bold statement in such a magnificent way.

Making our way up to the cross on top of Cross Mountain

Looking at the cross I began to wonder, "How are these people so humble while at the same time so mighty and bold in their actions? Why was I so resistant? Why was I so opposed to coming here? What had I really been fighting? Was it my pride or a feeling of rejection?" Jesus had called Judy here, through His mother. Just like the twelve disciples, she had followed without a question. I had not made this trip easy for her. I wondered what I would have actually done if I had been one of the names given to Terri instead of Judy. Would I have ignored this? I was pretty sure I knew the answer to that. Looking around, in deep thought, I caught a glimpse of Judy walking about, taking everything in all by herself. In a few minutes, I walked over to her, put my arms around her and we hugged each other on top of Cross Mountain for a long time, each deep in our own thoughts.

I knew there was something special about Judy from the very first time I met her. She was so full of life and had that "joy thing" I was missing. She had very close friends and a family she cared deeply about. She had a lot of what I was missing. Here we were on top of a mountain, in a remote area of Yugoslavia, just days before our one year anniversary. I had wanted to forget about all of this and take off for an island vacation somewhere. I was beginning to be thankful that Judy had taken a firm stand in coming here. I eventually had given in, telling myself it was to make sure she didn't go off the deep end. The truth is I had fears, fears that did not have their origin in my love for Judy or even her desire for God and her honesty in seeking him. It was the fear of the unknown. I just did not know where I would fit in the aftermath and this speaks more to my own insecurity than anything else.

I always felt like I got better than I deserved with Judy. The failure of my first marriage had left large wounds when it came to trust and I know I had been guilty of putting blame on Judy for things she never did or even thought. I realized I had brought a lot of baggage with me when I first met Judy. It had robbed me of having the kind of relationship I really wanted; it had robbed Judy too. I wanted to be the kind of man she needed me to be but I couldn't let go of my need to be in control. It was difficult for me to abandon myself to anything and so I held out on her too.

I had not come to Medjugorje to say "See, I told you so." I had taken Bob's advice to "Just come and see and be open." I was here but, still, I was not expecting anything of significance to really happen. I was happy just to be getting a retreat from the world as we know it. There was a hint that maybe I was beginning to connect with something that was missing in me and maybe I was beginning to feel more comfortable about all of this. Judy said she was at peace and felt like her confusion about whether God was with her or cared about what she was going through had already been answered. She was happy to be here, simply because she had been asked to be here. I told myself that I came to protect her but, in reality, it was my own insecurities and fears that I was trying to protect. I didn't want anything to change Judy. If coming here were to change her, where would that leave me?

I'm not a joiner. It's not that I am happier being alone but it's more that I'm really just not unhappy when I am alone, even for long periods. Judy, on the other hand, loved to join in and connect with everybody. This is one of the things that attracted me to her in the first place. It's also one of the things that fed my insecurities. It's not that I ever distrusted Judy, but, while she was connecting with everyone else in a room, I would often feel left out. She was so different from me in this way.

I had a lot of thoughts running around in my head. It was easy for me to understand why Judy would be invited. After the experience at Billy Graham's Crusade, it was also easy to understand why I was not. Even still, our morning walk up Cross Mountain had begun to open something up in me. All the prayers during our walk up the mountain had, in some ways, invited me into the life of Christ. It had been subtle and gradual, allowing me the time to draw upon my own experiences and thoughts all along the way. I'm not sure if I realized it at the time, but something was beginning to change in me. It was very humbling to stand in the midst of so many people praying and to reflect on the suffering of Jesus.

Not only had I been invited into this walk with Jesus, but the people of Medjugorje and the people I was traveling with had all invited me in. Somehow, by sharing in the experience of climbing the mountain and thinking about what Jesus had endured, I felt I had begun, in some way, to become a part of what Medjugorje was all about. The freedom in this place was so non-invasive and it simply revealed itself to you. It did not challenge me or make me uncomfortable in any way. It did not say, "You must believe." It said, "Just look around, listen, observe, feel and touch me." I privately thought to myself, "I am going to climb this mountain again before we go home. Barefoot!"

Medjugorje, in many ways, was like a puzzle and some of the parts and pieces had been put together over decades in time. Before coming here, I had wanted to make sure I knew nothing about this place. I had heard there were miracles occurring here but I didn't want to be preconditioned about what they were. Now that I had been here for almost a full twenty-four hours, I had begun to hear about how all the pieces of the puzzle had "coincidentally" come together to form this special place. There were different generations who had contributed to the mat of the puzzle. One generation had built this magnificent Cross in 1933, forty-eight years before the apparitions began. This thirty foot cross that weighed sixteen tons had been built as a monument to show the world their faith in Jesus. Now all these years later, people from all over the world were drawn like a magnet to this remote spot on the globe as a journey in their faith. Plans had been drawn up and construction on the church has begun in 1934. Forty seven years after this, the apparitions began. The church was so much larger than the people in this tiny village would ever need, but now the church was bursting out of its seams with multiple masses in a variety of languages every day. It did seem like the hand of God had been moving and preparing this place for almost fifty years. In August of 1984, The Virgin Mary told the children that, "The Cross was in God's plan when it was built." Everything seemed connected by the hand of God, by Divine Providence, and all had a common thread of "faith, hope and trust." It was mind boggling to realize that hundreds of thousands of people, from all over the world, had been here and walked this path every day long before we had arrived.

JUDY

On top of Cross Mountain, everyone had gone off in their own direction. I was in my own thoughts, just walking around quietly, taking everything in. I think it was a time for quiet reflection for most of us. Walking up Cross Mountain and contemplating on the pain and suffering that Christ had endured on his way to the cross had begun to bring everything into focus. There was a reason we all were here, and those reasons were as many and as varied as there were people. We could physically see and read some of the reasons as we walked about. There were hundreds of rock mounds with small wooden crosses stuck in them all over the top of the mountain. Some of the crosses had prayer petitions taped to them or photographs of love ones attached. Others had prayers written on the crosses themselves. There were prayers for healings, prayers for lost loved ones and also small memorials to loved ones who had died. These were all personal things that were on the hearts and minds of people who had come to Medjugorje, but I believed God's reason for us being here was to bring us all closer to Him. The Virgin Mary had told Terri that she was here in Medjugorje to bring people closer to her son. I was wondering if that might be happening to Don. He really hadn't talked to me very much about what he was thinking or feeling, but I could see he was softening up to the people in our group. Now that we were here, he seemed to be enjoying things and he seemed very relaxed on top of the mountain.

After about a half an hour, people in our group looked as if they were ready to head back down the mountain. Don found me and gave me a tight, long hug while we stood there together on top of Cross Mountain, not saying a word. In a few minutes, Terri caught up with us and took a treasured photograph of the two of us before we all decided it was time to go. The sun was much higher now and it was beginning to get hot on top of Cross Mountain. If we left now, we would be down the mountain in time for lunch.

Don and Judy on Cross Mountain, next to memorials to loved ones in background

When we arrived at the base of the mountain, we gathered to discuss when and where we would meet before we headed over to Ivan Dragicevic's house. Ivan was one of the older visionaries and we were excited that we were going to be able to hear him speak and hopefully answer some questions after our lunch. Several of us found an open cafe and ordered pizza. The atmosphere was lively and there were several young people, who looked to be college age, playing their guitars and singing with great enthusiasm. Everything was festive and everyone seemed very happy down in the village. We finished our lunch and decided to head on over to Ivan's house, hoping to get close enough to hear him talk about the messages. When we arrived at his house, a large crowd had already gathered and Ivan and his interpreter were standing on the porch steps, which were elevated above the crowd. This was our first real glimpse of any of the visionaries. The interpreter introduced himself and began translating Ivan's account of the apparition with the Virgin Mary from the day before, August 11th. I was so impressed with the patience and the sincerity coming from this young man, who was now twenty-five years old. He described how Mary was dressed, how she appeared and how long she had talked to them, as well as some of the questions they had asked her.

Ivan (visionary) on the left with his interpreter

Ivan said the Virgin Mary asked all to pray for her intentions, explaining that this helped her. Many people began to ask him if there were any comments about the Middle East conflict that was brewing at the time. Ivan's reply was that she always asked for her children to pray for peace but she had said nothing particular the night before. Ivan talked about the importance of forming prayer groups. He also said it was very important that we pray with our families and emphasized that Mary said family prayer should be our first priority of prayer. He also said that harmony in the home creates trust and to start this early in a child's life. He said it was harder to form the heart of a twenty-five year old. He said authority should be from love and that we should not humiliate children. Additionally he said that we should also limit the decisions of children and we should limit ourselves as well. He commented that, if we were disturbed by the youth, we should be disturbed about ourselves first. He talked about how, today, children would learn to use the television remote control before learning how to pray. We were encouraged to be responsible for the youth and first set a good example. He warned us to be aware of dangerous things affecting our youth, and said that instructions in school concerning religion were bad and should change. He also lamented that a child's friends have more influence on them than their parents and that parents should spend more time and give more love to their youth.

Many questions began flowing from the crowd, and he was incredibly tolerant of the questions I knew he had answered a thousand times before. I wasn't sure how he did this but we had been told that all of the visionaries displayed the same patience and grace with everyone who came to Medjugorje.

Below are just a few of the questions that we recorded:

Question: *"Are there any comments about non Catholics that don't follow the teachings of the Roman Catholic Church?"*

Ivan: *"Our Lady said she came here as the "Mother of All the World" and her messages are for all faiths and people."*

Young girl: *"Why do we fast?"*

Ivan: *"Fasting is a way of purifying the soul."*

Young girl: *"Thank you Ivan, for your work with youth."*

Question: *"How has seeing the Virgin Mary helped you with your prayer life?"*

Ivan: *"You must pray with the heart. Sometimes I have problems that interfere with prayer. I have to fast as it is my duty to relay the messages. I am like you. I have these problems in my mind when I am praying. My advantage is that I am able to bring these concerns directly to Our Lady in my prayers. She gives me direct encouragement, but in other ways I am just like you with my struggles. I read scripture and try to apply it to my life." He went on to make many comments about the importance of praying with our hearts.*

Question:	*"Do you pray for America?"*
Ivan:	*"I pray for the whole world."*

The last question was my favorite of the day. He was asked if Our Lady has been told when the world would end.

Ivan:	*"Our Lady says that she often learns more from people that come here than she knows for herself." There was an outburst of laughter with that comment.*

After about 40 minutes, Ivan concluded his talk and I remembered not just being impressed with his patience and humility, but also his humor at times.

After leaving Ivan's house we had some free time to walk around Medjugorje. Later, we met the others for the English Mass and afterwards we headed home for our evening meal.

It had been a long day and the climb up Cross Mountain had caused us all to want to turn in a little early this evening. Just as Don and I had drifted off to sleep, we woke up to a strong jolt and a rumbling sound. I jumped up and told Don that it felt like an earthquake. He rolled over and said, "No, It's just some people running down the stairs." In a few moments, we felt it again and both of us got up and went to the window to find almost everyone, including our host family, standing outside the building. It had, in fact, been a small earthquake, strong enough to startle those of us not used to them but not strong enough to do any damage. The rumbling we had heard was the earthquake and not people running down the stairs. I had never experienced an earthquake or even felt a tremor so I'm not sure how I was able to quickly discern what was going on. Several in our group were urging us to hurry out, while our host family was trying to erase everyone's fears. Out of precaution, we decided to join everyone outside and quickly left the building, with me yelling over my shoulder, "I knew it was an earthquake!" Once we were outside for ten minutes or so our host continued to assure everyone that we should all just go back to bed. There was a lot of nervous laughter once it was over but, eventually, everyone went back to their room and settled in. We did the same and thankfully we all slept through the night, with no more rumbles.

Judy content and enjoying the peace and
beauty of Medjugorje

He restores my soul; He guides
me in paths of righteousness for
His name's sake.

Psalms 23:3
New American Standard Bible

Chapter 10

Hope Dashed

JUDY

*T*he morning of our third day started out much like the *day before with the exception that it wasn't quite as early. We gathered in the dining room for breakfast, talked about the day's events and what we would be doing. We still had not received our luggage or any word as to where it was or when it might arrive. Everyone continued to share and help each other with what they had. I began to wonder if this was part of God's plan for us too. Somehow, we were all making out fine and no one seemed to go without anything and everyone's needs appeared to be getting met. I thought about the first night when we met in the dining room to discuss everyone's needs. This process of helping each other and sharing our belongings had caused us to quickly bond together as a group. It had also helped us get to know each other as individuals a* *lot faster. Although we would have loved for our luggage to have arrived by now, we were quickly learning we could do without a lot of the things we had packed as "necessities." It was beginning to feel like we were a family of sorts - lots of brothers and sisters, cousins, aunts and uncles, mothers and fathers and grandparents. It was really interesting having all the different ages and to be able to hear the different perspectives each brought to Medjugorje.*

There was Henry and his wife Anita, a couple who appeared to be in their sixties. Henry and Anita were solid Catholics, and from the first time we met Henry he had begun talking of this place called Fatima that a family member had once visited. We learned from Henry that Fatima was an earlier Marian Apparition site, at the turn of the 20th Century in Portugal. Henry's relative had visited Fatima and Henry had always remembered his account of what had happened there in 1917 with great details. There were many similarities between Fatima and Medjugorje. Just as Mary had appeared to six children here in Medjugorje, she had suddenly appeared to three children in Fatima. As in Medjugorje, the people of Fatima had not believed the children at first. The children in Fatima had asked the Virgin Mary to help the others believe that they were not lying. The Virgin Mary had promised the Children that on October 13th, at noon, there would be a great public miracle so all would believe them. It had been pouring rain for days and the ground was soaking wet and soggy. The rain continued pouring down on October 13th but still at least 70,000 people came, including atheists and the non-religious, and all stood in the rain. Secular newspapers from all over the world were there, including The New York Times, to report on what the children had promised would occur. When the children arrived, they received both adulation as well as mockery, from those who had made their way there. When noon came and nothing happened, some laughed and ridiculed them and joked that the Blessed Mother was not very punctual. Suddenly the rain stopped and the sun came out and all could look directly at the sun without it hurting their eyes. While they were all looking at the sun, it began to rotate like a pinwheel casting a variety of shades of colors all over the people and the land. The sun appeared to plunge towards the earth three different times, frightening the crowd and many, including non-believers, fell to their knees, pleading for God's mercy. After about twelve minutes of this phenomenon, the sun went back to its natural place in a clear sky. Their clothes and the ground around them had become completely dry. Every person there testified to seeing the sun dance. Many non-believers dropped onto their knees begging for forgiveness. Everyone there confirmed what had happened.

Many people in Medjugorje had reported seeing the "Miracle of the Sun," as well. In Fatima, there were some differences, but many reported seeing the sun spin and move positions in the sky. Others had seen the Eucharist Host (the round wafer used in Holy Communion) cover the sun and they would be able to look at the sun for extended periods, without any harm to their eyes. At our first meeting at Lois's house, before we left for Medjugorje, Henry had brought five scapulars that had been given to him by his relative who had brought them back from Fatima. At that meeting, he had explained these scapulars had been blessed in Fatima and he had held on to them for years. I had never heard of or seen a scapular, so I had no idea what these handmade objects were. The scapular was composed of two separate, small pieces of square cloth that were connected by a lengthy piece of fabric, much like a long flat woven shoe string. The small, square pieces of cloth were brown and they had a hand stitched blue cross in the center of each piece of cloth. Henry didn't explain to us what a scapular really was because it seemed all the Catholics already knew and Henry had assumed we were all Catholic. It was only later that I learned these scapulars represented a particular devotion and, in this case, it was to the Virgin Mary. Henry said he had been compelled to bring these scapulars with him and had prayed that God would show him whom to give them to. As he went around the room, passing them out, he had no idea he had chosen the only five non-Catholics going on this trip. This was just the beginning of many coincidences, but I was clearly beginning to under-stand these things as "God nods" - those little things that happen along the way that give you affirmation you are on God's radar and have not been forgotten.

Henry was definitely one of those traveling in our group hoping to see a miracle and he had his heart set on seeing the "Miracle of the Sun," just like his relative had in Fatima so many years ago. This particular morning, Henry was talking about it again and you could see the longing in his heart to receive this one special grace while here.

I had been basking in this simple lifestyle of Medjugorje for just a few days now but I had already begun to make some interesting observations. Everything here was centered on the church, the prayers and the messages the Virgin Mary was giving the world though these six visionaries. There were no bars, at the time, where people might gather in the evening to watch a football game. There was no beach or swimming pools where we could sunbathe during down time. There were no big name stars coming into town for a concert. There was no entertainment at all. Everything was centered on faith. The people turned to God here without shame. The absence of the typical distractions we had back home allowed you to just soak in the life of this parish. It was not unusual to see a group of people praying together along the sidewalks or connecting with complete strangers to share their wonderful experiences.

When we were in Medjugorje, we were surrounded by such strong faith all the time; it was impossible not to feel the presence of God. In truth, I felt it the minute we got here. It's hard to explain, but it was like the atmosphere was full of goodness and grace. Beyond everything else going on here with the appearance of the Virgin Mary, I think Medjugorje offered us some insight into seeking God's presence. It's found when you are surrounded by people of strong faith and in a quiet place without the usual things distracting and calling you away. I was already falling in love with the village. Its simplicity, beauty and peaceful holiness were offering me something I had never been exposed to before. I wanted to take it all home with me, especially the church. Don and I had started visiting churches back home, at one point, but I had never felt the way I felt here in any of the other churches. Here at St. James, the level of reverence and holiness was more than I had experienced anywhere.

I began to make other observations about the people who lived here - the true families of Medjugorje. They have so little in comparison to what we have in America, but they seem to have everything they needed. They were poor by our standards but it did not look like poverty. They seem very proud and happy. They have their church, their families, their farms and now they have the Virgin Mary and thousands of people coming here every week from all four corners of the world. Their simple way of life has been turned upside down by all of this. Still, they greeted all of us so warmly and seemed to go out of their way to make us feel at home. It was not unusual for a local elderly woman to stand up in church to offer a pilgrim her seat. Everything seemed to center around love and sacrifice. There was so much to appreciate here and I was learning from these people without realizing it. It felt like it was rubbing off on all of us. Just being here made you want to be more patient, more loving and kind. I wondered how long Medjugorje could possibly stay like this as more and more people found their way here. At the time of our visit, it had been nine years since the Virgin Mary first appeared to the children and only a few shops and restaurants had opened up to serve those coming in. I really hoped it wouldn't change too much over time.

By this time, Don and I had both bought a Rosary from one of the local shops and had become very familiar with the prayer we had heard so often now. I really had a hard time praying the Rosary, in the beginning, because I had always thought of it as a prayer to Mary instead of Jesus. I strongly believed that we were to pray to Jesus and only to Jesus, based on what I understood the Bible to say. Some of my new Catholic friends explained to me that it was more like asking the Blessed Mother to pray for us, just like we would ask our earthly mothers or friends to pray for us. We are all intercessors for each other but, because of Mary's special relationship to her son, her prayers were believed to be very strong prayers. We have no problem asking others to pray for us, so this was no different. Then I had problems with the repetitiveness of the prayers. I was citing Matthew 6:7 in scripture that tells us not to pray using vain repetition. My new friends explained that the emphasis was on the "vain" repetition of "many words" which were designed to impress people. After reading the scripture again it was clear to me that this was the real intent of the message. The Rosary was not said to impress people, like the Pharisees did in the Bible, rather these repetitive prayers were more of a meditation that kept us in prayer longer. Through this Rosary prayer, we spent more time meditating on the life of Jesus. I could see that. To say a full Rosary generally took about an hour. We would usually say a part of this prayer each day, which would take about twenty minutes. I couldn't remember a time when I stayed in prayer for five solid minutes, much less twenty, and usually my prayer was full of pleas for God to help me in some way. This prayer really was different and caused you to spend time meditating on all the important events during Christ's earthly life instead of your own needs. It was much the same as praying the "Stations of the Cross." The purpose was to simply spend time with God in prayer, remembering Him. Spending time with Him, remembering His life, drew us closer to Him. I had begun to experience all of this for myself so, not only had I come to terms with this "one more Catholic thing," I was now feeling drawn to it.

The first thing Don and I had planned to do this morning was to walk down to St. James to meet two nuns who were visiting from California. The day before, someone in our group had met them and had learned they had a healing ministry. We were told they would be in front of St. James at 9 a.m. I was surprised when Don began to ask questions about them and even more surprised when he said he wanted to go meet them. Don would never have been open to this a few days ago, but I could tell he was opening up. He wanted to talk to these nuns and ask them to pray for his sister. Don's sister had been poisoned by a faulty product made by a Japanese pharmaceutical company who had cut the amino acid L-tryptophan with an ingredient that had caused irreparable physical damage and death to many who had taken the product. His sister had terrible health problems because of this, but she was considered to be one of the lucky ones since she was a survivor. I, too, was interested in meeting the sisters, although I wasn't sure if it was anything more than simple curiosity

DON

We arrived at the courtyard of St. James around 9 a.m. with a few of the people in our group who had met with the sisters the day before. They were dressed in what I supposed were their summer habits, a below the knees black skirt, short sleeve white blouse and the nun headpiece, which had a much shorter than normal veil. They were waiting on us with warm and welcoming smiles that seemed to let you know that praying with and for others was a labor of love for them. We talked to them for a few minutes and exchanged pleasantries and then Sister Delores, who had the gift of healing, began to ask us a few questions. She first asked Judy if she had any special prayer request, which seemed to catch Judy off guard. I think Judy had felt that we were coming to pray for my sister and had not really given any thought to prayers or concerns for herself. Judy kind of stumbled around saying something about her mother who had passed away three years earlier.

Judy's mother had died suddenly two days before Christmas, while visiting her brother in Atlanta. Judy received the call from her brother shortly after she had been taken to the hospital, but by the time Judy was able to catch a flight to Atlanta and get to the hospital, her mother was unconscious and on life-support. The doctors had not given the family any hope she would recover, but Judy had hoped she would at least wake up long enough for her to say goodbye, but that never happened. When it came time for the doctors to turn off her life-support, Judy could not face it and left the room rather than stay there. Later, that turned out to be a decision she had regretted. I don't know what Judy was thinking, but I think she wanted to have some sort of connection with her mother and maybe an opportunity to say goodbye here. I know Judy didn't even have the words to express what she wanted exactly. I remember the nuns looked at each other and Sister Delores told Judy that it was an unusual prayer request but that they would pray for this. The Sisters prayed with Judy for a few minutes and then smiled at her. Judy thanked them and stepped away.

When the Sisters came to me, I told them I wanted prayer for my sister, who was very ill. They asked me a few questions about her and then said they would pray for her in absentia, explaining I would stand in on behalf of my sister as they laid hands on me to pray for her. Sister Delores asked me to come and stand between her and the other nun and they asked permission to place their hands on my back and across my heart. I answered, "Yes" and they began to pray for my sister. Almost immediately I felt a tremendous heat surge through my body; I closed my eyes and began quietly praying for my sister along with them. As they continued praying, I began to get a visual image in my mind but it was not of my sister. It was of Judy's mother. She was kneeling in front of the Virgin Mary with her arms around Mary and her mother's head was resting against Mary's lap. Her mother's head was turned towards me and she smiled. As Judy's mother was looking at me and smiling, the Virgin Mary was lovingly caressing her hair. I had only known Judy's mother for a short time, when she was in her seventies, but in this vision she was much younger, more like in her early thirties, but there was no doubt this was Judy's mother. The vision was so clear and the message of the image was so strong, I was shocked. I never had anything like this happen to me before. I had no idea why I received this image rather than Judy, but there was a strong message of love and a secure feeling that Judy's mother was in a good place and at peace.

Soon the prayers ended and I opened my eyes, still wondering what had just happened. Without moving their hands, Sister Delores asked me what prayers I would like for myself. This also caught me off guard and I really didn't know what to say. I was not comfortable with people praying for me, so I told the Sisters that I came here really asking for nothing but I would like to have peace with all that was occurring here and also peace with myself. I honestly felt if I could just find peace, that this, in and of itself, would be a tremendous blessing for me. My words did not come close to conveying what I really wanted to ask for but couldn't express. I couldn't bring myself to ask for the prayer I felt I needed the most, the prayer that Christ would accept me. I was still carrying that horrifying secret that I couldn't bear to share with anyone. I also told them that I had experienced back problems before coming to Medjugorje. The Sisters nodded in agreement and began praying specific prayers for my peace and good health. Within a few minutes, they ended their prayers and Sister Delores's companion said she had something she wanted to share with me. She shared with me that she had the gift of visions and that very often when she was in prayer with someone she would receive a vision for them. As she continued, she said that while they had been praying she had received a vision for me. In her vision she saw me and Jesus facing each other on two separate shores. She said we were separated by a large body of water and that the water was flowing back and forth between us. She explained she could not interpret the vision but if I prayed about this she was sure Jesus would reveal the meaning to me.

Any peace I had been praying for immediately vanished with what she just described to me. I didn't need to pray about its meaning. I was pretty sure I knew exactly what it meant. I had been here before. In one swift moment, any hope I had begun to sense instantly disappeared. All my doubts came flooding back. The vision was more than disappointing to me and I began questioning why she would tell me such a thing. After all, she didn't know me. Why would she tell me something so upsetting? I knew she was sincere in giving me this vision and that she had no way of knowing how upsetting it was for me to hear. There was no way she could know my well-guarded secret. That this vision simply lined itself up with the experience I had at the Billy Graham Crusade. I understood her vision. It represented the painful separation and rejection I had received there too. Any hope, peace or glimmer of joy was drained out of me, in an instant, as I recalled that painful memory I had never shared with a soul.

> The LORD is close to the brokenhearted
> and saves
> those who are crushed in spirit.
>
> Psalm 34:18
> New International Version

Chapter 11

The Secret

DON

It was the second night that Judy and I had attended the Billy Graham Crusade a few years ago in Tallahassee. The night before this I had listened to Billy Graham's message intently and at the end of the service, I felt called to go down to the altar with many of the others to re-dedicate my life, yet I had resisted. I told myself that I wanted to make sure I was serious and that I wasn't just getting caught up in the emotion of the moment. On this second night, I felt my spirit called again so I stepped out and began walking down to the floor on the very last verse of "Just as I Am." This was the exact same song that drew me to answer God's call at the age of fourteen, when I was baptized. As I descended the stairs and stepped on the floor and began to move closer to the stage, I was overcome with the strongest feeling of rejection I had ever felt. Something came all over me and there seemed to be a barrier between me and the stage that I couldn't go through. My whole being was screaming, "Go back! Go back! You have no right to be here! You do not belong!" I was shocked and mortified and I didn't know what to do. I suddenly felt terribly sick to my stomach. I stopped walking and just stood there, no longer able to approach the stage. All the others continued to move past me as my doubts possessed me and left me frozen. I could hardly move as I dropped my head in this defeat and rejection and turned to go back to my seat. When I got back to where Judy was sitting I was anxious to leave. Judy wanted to know what had happened. She could tell something was wrong and she was confused as to why I had returned. She continued to ask me what had happened when we got in the car. I just couldn't tell her so I told her I couldn't talk about it right then. She asked me if I would tell her later and I said I would, but I never did. If she ever brought it up again, I would just shake my head and somehow she knew it was just too personal.

I had been carrying this around with me for years. I tried to bury it but whenever anything "spiritual" or particularly painful would happen, it would raise its head. In fact, this was the reason for all my questions about whether the Virgin Mary had asked for Judy Powell or Judy Bailey.

Perhaps if she had asked for Judy Bailey, there might be some hope for me in all of this. In truth, perhaps this was the reason I had put up such a stink about coming. Maybe I didn't want to get close to something that had already rejected me a long time ago. "My God," I thought, "I had just crossed over a giant ocean to get here." I knew it was Judy that had been invited but, without realizing it, I had begun to hope there was something here that might blot out that painful memory for me and give me a little hope too.

Dear God, the feelings of rejection and separation from Christ was happening here all over again. Judy was just a few feet away and I didn't want to face the same kind of questions again. I didn't want her to ask me what was wrong. I had been in a hopeful place on the way over to visit the nuns. I was sure Judy would pick up on my mood change and she would have endless questions. At home I could go hide to get away from the questions. Here I was in a group of people and there was no good place to go hide and somehow that seemed to make things even worse.

After lunch, we were all planning a bus ride over to hear Fr. Jozo talk about the early days of the apparitions. I had been looking forward to that, too, but now I just wanted to go home. I was certain a priest wouldn't be able to say anything that could change the way I was feeling. I was even feeling a twinge of embarrassment and maybe shame thinking my well hidden secret must have been revealed to these nuns. I exchanged addresses with the two Sisters, thanked them for their prayers and we parted company.

As I looked around the church courtyard everything seemed to be in slow motion as I started taking it all in. I could see others experiencing joy with such ease. For me, there was just a big void of emotion. I was trying to understand why I always had such a hard time experiencing true joy for any length of time. It always seemed to elude me. It felt like a curse and something I wanted but just couldn't have. To me, it seemed like I couldn't get close to anything good without something rising up to kill the joy of it. This experience was no different, and the more joy I saw in others, the more painful it was for me. I didn't go to Medjugorje consciously looking for anything specific. Still, up until this moment, I had started to feel a sense of joy here. A connection had begun to form to this place, the people here and especially with many of the people we had been traveling with. Now, I wasn't sure what to do with what had just happened. I knew I had sin in my life. I was fully aware that I was far from perfect but, after these first few days, I had started hoping I would find a way to break though this spirit of resistance that had always haunted me. I was a bit confused because none of this really coincided with the way I had felt about Christ. A very long time ago

I had accepted that Jesus was the Son of God. Even still, this had done very little to change the way I lived my life and it had not removed the lack of joy I felt. I could be out having a good time with Judy and it seemed like a switch would turn off telling me it was time for the good time to be over. It would happen suddenly and Judy could not understand what happened. I wasn't able to explain it to her either. I couldn't even understand it myself. At this particular moment, I felt like I was headed in that direction again. I had enjoyed almost three days here and the vision the nun had given me had triggered my 'joy-kill switch.' I was starting to feel anxiety, thinking this was the beginning of other things that might go wrong. I wanted to kick something or at least find a place to get away from everyone.

As bad as this experience was, I still somehow felt some comfort about the prayers for my sister and the vision I had seen of Judy's mother. I knew I needed to share this with Judy and wondered if it would comfort her or cause her to question why someone like me, who had resisted all of this, would receive a spiritual vision of any significance. I was questioning that myself. Either way, I knew this was something I needed to share with her, but I also knew I couldn't have that conversation right now. I was trying to find something in me that might be in harmony with things that were going on in Medjugorje, and I really wasn't sure it was possible now. I was beginning to feel like a ball tossed up between Heaven and Hell. Prior to all of this, I had not been looking for a "spiritual" connection. Knowing about Jesus and accepting Him as the Son of God was one thing, but to actually believe the things of Heaven and the things of Earth could be connected in some tangible way was another thing altogether. I know I didn't think this was possible before coming to Medjugorje. Somehow, in spite of the nun's vision, which was still haunting me, I knew I had also experienced a peek into the "other side" with my vision of Judy's mother. It was like a veil that separated the two worlds had been temporarily lifted and I got to peer in and see the "other side." On the one hand, I was in awe and my spirit was lifted to connect with something spiritual, something as alive as Judy's mother was in my vision. On the other hand, my heart was heavy from the personal separation I was realizing once again, due to the nun's vision. My vision was for Judy's comfort. The nun's vision was to reaffirm that deep part of me that knew all about my separation from God. Feelings of rejection and those familiar feelings of not belonging were beginning to set in. I didn't know what I was going to do but I desperately wished I had a place where I could get away from this throng of people around me. I was beginning to think I really didn't belong here after all and I had just crashed a party that I hadn't been invited to. I had somehow let my guard down and had begun to open up to everything in Medjugorje. Worse, I had begun to think I was becoming a part of this, and now this aching reality hit me squarely in the face. I felt resentment growing in me again. There was nothing I could do. I was stuck here with all these happy, hopeful, peaceful people and I wanted nothing more than to find a beer or some other means of an escape.

I don't remember how the remainder of the morning progressed, up until the time for us to meet the bus to Tihaljina to go hear Fr. Jozo Zovko. One thing was for sure, my attitude was declining by the hour and my desire to go was gone by the time the bus arrived. The only good thing going for me at this point was the fact that Judy wasn't pressing me to answer any questions about the nun's vision. At least, temporarily, I received a reprieve. It seemed that everyone, including Judy, was excited to be going to hear Fr. Jozo, with the exception of me. When the bus arrived, I was at least happy to see it was a new bus with the high profile big glass all the way around. At least the bus ride over would give me a chance to chill out and cool off in a comfortable air-conditioned bus.

JUDY

Visiting and praying with the nuns this morning at St. James was a nice experience for me, even though I had begun to feel a little embarrassed about asking for such a strange request regarding my mother. I was a little surprised at myself, actually, and wondered why I asked for this, when there were others things I could have asked them to pray for. Looking back on this, I don't know why I had not thought to ask for prayers to have a child. My sadness over all my miscarriages had, in a very real way, started me on this journey. It was after praying so hard that nothing would go wrong during my pregnancies and then experiencing multiple miscarriages, along with the ectopic pregnancy, that I had begun to feel so abandoned by God. All that sadness had disappeared here and I was simply in complete awe of everything we were experiencing together as a group.

I was excited we were all going to be able to travel to a town after lunch called Tihaljina which was about 35 km from Medjugorje and about a 40 minute drive. The purpose of this trip was to hear Fr. Jozo talk about the early days of the apparitions. Fr. Jozo was the priest in charge at St. James in Medjugorje when the first apparition occurred on June 24, 1981. During the first days, Fr. Jozo had been very disturbed by the children claiming that the Virgin Mary had been appearing to them. He had quizzed them repeatedly. He recorded his interviews with them, trying to see if he could catch them slipping up or contradicting themselves. As word spread, thousands of people had begun to flood into the vil-

lage and were walking past his church up to the hill where the apparitions were taking place. By Sunday, June 28th, 15,000 people had gathered to witness the children as they received their visit from the Virgin Mary. Alone in St. James, Fr. Jozo had turned to prayer, trying to understand all the events taking place in his parish and asking God what he should do. As he was praying, he heard a voice telling him, "Go out and protect the children." He quickly left the altar and headed to the back of the church, and the moment he opened the door the children came running up to him crying and asking for him to hide them from the police. After consoling the children, he placed them in a room in the rectory, near the church, and then he returned to the church. Soon the police came looking for the children and when they asked Fr. Jozo if he had seen the children, he replied "yes" and looked away from the church. The police quickly left, running in the direction that Fr. Jozo had looked. After this, Fr. Jozo came to believe in the visions and the children.

Within days, the communist authorities in nearby Citluk decided to take action, fearing that this might be some sort of cover for a political plot. They gathered the children and questioned them intensively at a police station in nearby Mostar. Later, a doctor examined the children and declared them all to be normal and healthy. Completely frustrated, the authorities called Fr. Jozo in and ordered him to stop the people from gathering. Fr. Jozo simply did not respond. They told him that if these gatherings did not stop, he would be held personally accountable. Next, the authorities sent in a state psychiatrist to observe the children during the next apparition on the hill. The psychiatrist went to the hill, but did not file a report. She was seen leaving the hill, visibly shaken. Next the authorities came in and forbade the children from going to Podboro Hill, but the Virgin Mary continued to appear to them each day, regardless of where they were. No matter what the authorities tried to do to stop all of this, the people continued to come. To make matters worse, they were reporting miraculous healings. Within a few weeks, the authorities realized that they were going to have to take stronger measures, so they dispatched special police from Sarajevo to surround the village of Medjugorje. The police blocked off all the entrances to and from Medjugorje and called all the men of the village to report to military service. They were ordered to encircle Cross Mountain and Podboro Hill with orders not to allow anyone to pass through. During this time, the police were also recording sermons of the priest to see if they were delivering any anti-Communist messages. It was a very difficult time for everyone, especially the children. At one point, the authorities ordered Fr. Jozo to close the church but he refused. On August 17th, soldiers were sent in by air and land and helicopters began to hover over the village. The police, who had blocked the roads to Medjugorje, formed circles around the village. In front of St. James there were two lines of people. One was the soldiers with guns and dogs and the other was made up of the people with Rosaries in their hands, who were waiting to enter the church. The people of Medjugorje began to pray and continued to pray for hours. Neither line would move. Close to sunset something happened that shocked everyone. An order from Belgrade, the capital, arrived allowing people to enter the church. This was the first time in forty years that the primarily atheist Communist regime had ever reversed a decision like this. Still, the harassments continued, but, eventually, the authorities began to realize that it was impossible to stop the children from reporting their apparitions with the Virgin Mary. Fr. Jozo, however, was not so fortunate. The soldiers arrested him and gave him a horrible beating. He was given a mock trial and then sentenced to three and a half years in prison. During his prison stay, it was reported that the guards could not keep his cell door locked, much like Paul in the Bible. Once they moved him from one cell to another, the old cell door lock would work but not his new one. After his arrest, there was a tremendous outpouring of world wide support for Fr. Jozo. After 18 months he was released, but on the condition that he could not go back to his church in Medjugorje, and that was why we were now traveling some 35 km away to his new church in Tihaljina. Fortunately for us, these harassments had suddenly discontinued after seven years, just two years before our trip. The popular belief was that the government had realized how much money the pilgrims were actually bringing into their country and decided this was now a financial benefit to them.

Our group was eager to meet Fr. Jozo and hear him tell the story of Medjugorje first hand. We had gathered to wait outside our place when the travel coach finally arrived. While we were waiting, the sun was high in the sky and beating down on us and it was an extremely hot day. Once the doors to the bus opened, the bus driver stepped out and pulled our guide, Dragan, off to the side, out of our hearing. The conversation went on for a while and even though they were speaking Croatian, I could tell that Dragan was not really happy. He seemed to be very concerned about something. It appeared that Dragan was asking a lot of questions, but whatever the questions were the answer to each question was "No." Within a few minutes Dragan, walked toward us and asked for our attention. He explained to us there was a problem with the bus and that the air conditioner was not working. Evidently, they had tried to fix it earlier but they needed certain parts that would not arrive until the next day. They had also looked for other buses but they were all in use and this was the only transportation available at this time that could take us to Tihaljina. If we wanted to see Fr. Jozo, *this was our only option, because this would be the only time he would be meeting with an English speaking group all week. Dragan explained it would be very uncomfortable because the windows would not go down except in an emergency, but he promised all of us that it would be worth it. If we wanted to go, we would need to leave right away.*

Don's immediate reaction was, "You gotta be kidding me!" (except, he didn't say it quite that nicely). To say he was disgruntled about our situation was putting it mildly and he didn't seem to mind who knew it. He thought the fact that it was 110 degrees outside constituted an emergency and he thought they should knock out a few windows, just to make it bearable. The news of our bus didn't seem to faze anyone else and I was beginning to get embarrassed that Don wanted to make such a fuss about it. I know I gave him one of my famous looks that said "knock it off," but that only made it worse because he looked at me and said loudly, "What? Am I supposed to be O.K. with this?" I was trying to be discrete and not involve any of the others in our private tift.Don, on the other hand, was put out and he didn't care who heard him. Once he got on the bus, you would have to be blind not to notice how angry he was. I didn't know what had come over him. I knew it was going to be a hot bus trip over but I thought he was way overreacting to this. I had noticed that after we had left the Sisters this morning, and during lunch, he had seemed distracted but I just thought he was probably thinking about the vision the nun had given him. Little did I know, that was exactly what had triggered this mood. At the time, I had no way of knowing why that would have upset him. There was nothing I had heard in the vision that would have given me a clue that anything was wrong.

As we began to settle in our seats, everyone still seemed to be in a great mood, except Don; he was beginning to make me feel very uncomfortable. We had just barely pulled out of Medjugorje when one of the young women in our group, who had been fanatically committed to praying the Rosary over and over, suggested we pray one now. Don looked at me, rolled his eyes and said, "If she says 'let's pray a Rosary,' one more time, I am going to take her Rosary and wrap it around her neck." I was horrified and looked around to see if anyone had heard him. I had no idea what was going on with him, but he was in such a foul mood that all I wanted to do was to get away from him. I decided to turn outward in my seat, toward others in our group, and conversed with those around me for the rest of the trip.

Beloved, do not trust every spirit but test
the spirits to see whether they
belong to God

1 John 4:1a
The New American Bible

Chapter 12

Father Jozo

DON

The bus ride had been more miserable than I had imagined. I was feeling the heat for sure, not just from the weather but also from Judy. I knew she thought I was overreacting to the bus's air conditioner breaking down but it was so much more than just that. She couldn't possibly know what was going on inside of me. There was no way I could put into words what I was feeling. There was that overpowering feeling of not really belonging here that had originally haunted me in the first place. I was feeling it again, and now with a vengeance. I kept playing it over and over again in my mind how the priest and other pilgrims and even the visionaries had said that "no one comes uninvited to Medjugorje. We have all been called and there is a reason why everyone is here." Others had said, "It is no coincidence that we are here." It would be nice to believe that but I didn't really believe it applied to me. I, on the other hand, had this gulf between me and Jesus that was too big. I felt empty and numb and I was wishing this bus was taking me to the airport and not to Tihaljina.

As the bus pulled up to the Church of the Immaculate Conception in Tihaljina, we all were eager to get out of this sweatbox, none more ready than me. A new surrounding would at least provide me with a distraction I needed in order to escape my thoughts. Departing the bus, I now turned my attention to the design of the church standing directly in front of me. Looking at the church, I noticed it had more architectural style than St. James did. I wanted more time to look at the church but everyone was in a hurry to get inside to find a seat. The church was already full with other English speaking groups from America, Great Britain and Ireland. There were only a few scattered seats, so it was necessary for our group to split up to find individual seats. Dragan was correct in telling us that we had no time to delay in leaving. In just a few more minutes, we would have found ourselves sitting in the aisles, on the stone floor or ushered up to sit on the steps leading up to the altar. At the moment, that would not have been a good thing for me. Some of those in our group found seats up near the front, while Judy and I found a couple of seats together about halfway back on the right side of the main entry aisle. Just as we had found at St. James, there were few creature comforts inside the church. There was the stone floor, high ceilings, wooden pews with no cushions and a horizontal trim board at the top of the backrest making sure you could not lean back and fall asleep. And, of course, there was no air conditioning.

Once we were settled in our seats, I began to turn my attention to our surroundings. Examining the architecture inside the church was a natural way for me to distract my thoughts and to help cool down my disposition. Immediately my attention was drawn to the left of the altar where I saw one of the most beautiful statues of the Virgin Mary I had ever seen. I had heard from others earlier about the beauty of this statue but no one had conveyed just how truly beautiful it was. The statue was called "Our Lady of Grace" and she was standing with her foot on the serpent, representing the devil I was sure, and above her head was a crown of 12 stars. On our way into the church, we had been given a postcard with the image of this statue on it and a healing prayer on the back.

People continued piling into the church and finding space on the floor to sit. The last ones finally entered and the large doors were closed behind them. Up unto this point, the open back doors had been providing a bit of a cross breeze from a few high windows that were also open. The ride over had sweated out a lot of my venom and the change of location was helping provide continued relief. Watching people enter in had taken some time and, fortunately, the activity had gotten my mind off of my rotten condition. The church was packed and overflowing and I began to realize how amazingly quiet it had suddenly gotten, in spite of the large crowd. I began to look at the card I had been given and turned it over to read the healing prayer on the back. Reading the card, I wondered if a simple prayer could actually heal you. If so, I needed it badly.

We had heard from others we had met that Fr. Jozo's message had been life changing for many and many people had converted. I was curious about what would be said that could have such a powerful impact. After three days, my impressions had run full circle and at this point I was not sure whether any of this was going to have a lasting effect on me or not. It was a lot to absorb in just three days. It's strange how your mind can accept certain things as truth and not others. Whether the Virgin Mary was appearing here or not I wasn't sure, but I knew something was going on here. I knew we would not even be here if Terri, Mary and Karen had not seen the Virgin Mary themselves. Terri and the others had testified to this and she had no reason to make this up. Terri had no way of knowing about Judy's prayer, and then there was Judy's dream. Everything connected like dots and I could not discount the picture that was coming into view. Some people felt it was the overwhelming amount of prayer that was responsible for the miracles and amazing graces that seemed to be pouring out on people here, and not necessarily the apparitions. Whatever people wanted to believe, it was hard to ignore the good fruits. People's lives were being changed, marriages were saved, people were being healed and faith was being restored. All but mine - I still didn't know how I fit in to any of this. Every time I thought I was beginning to feel a connection, something pulled the rug out from under me. But here I was, sitting in this church, still trying to make sense of what was going on in me. It occurred to me that just forgetting about it would be the simplest thing to do. That's what Judy said she had decided to do when she was so confused and said her fateful prayer. Maybe that's what I needed to do. Just give it up. Quit worrying about it. The truth is I hadn't been worrying about any of this before we came here. Before, I was fine. At least I thought I was.

As we continued to wait for Fr. Jozo's talk to begin, I started looking around again and watching what people were doing and observing how they were acting. Just sitting in this large group of people could ignite my senses in a way that can be revealing as well as troubling. A lot of people were praying. Some simply sat in their pews and bowed their heads, while others knelt, seemingly steeped in deep prayer. It was a great place to watch people but I began to realize I was being an observer again rather than a participant. I was wondering what was going on with them as they prayed and I also began to wonder why they were so caught up in prayer and I wasn't. I had never been one to do a lot of praying. I guess I figured God knew what was on my mind anyway. As I was observing all of this, I found myself wondering, "What was the point of all of this. Why do we need to spend so much time in prayer? Why the mystery? Why does Mary only reveal herself to the six children and not everyone? Why do we have to have faith anyway?" I was also wondering what these people were getting out of their prayers. "Why couldn't God just reveal everything to us? Why did he talk in parables?" Before, I wasn't thinking any of this but now I wanted to know. There were so many mysteries. On the one hand, there were all these seekers spending hours in prayer and meditation. Then you had these six children who were just out minding their own business, playing one afternoon and the Virgin Mary appears to them and begins to share heavenly messages. That didn't seem fair. They weren't out seeking God. Suddenly, a priest entered the altar area, followed by a young woman, which fortunately interrupted my frenetic thoughts. I assumed that this was Fr. Jozo.

JUDY

Applause broke out as Father Jozo and his interpreter walked out to the altar. His interpreter was a young woman and she began to simply beam in appreciation. Fr. Jozo, however, seemed to be a little uncomfortable with the loud and long applause and humbly nodded his head and put his hands up in an effort to quiet the applause. This only made everyone applaud louder. Fr. Jozo was a nice looking man but he was much younger than I had expected. He was a Franciscan Priest and wore the traditional simple brown robe and white rope belt. It was obvious he was uncomfortable with this form of adulation and he continued his protest. The crowd finally began to accept and settle down and his interpreter began to speak. "Good afternoon and welcome to the Church of the Immaculate Conception in Tihaljina. I am excited for you to come here and hear the words of Father Jozo Zovko. We give thanks to God, our Father, for this time with you and pray that you are blessed by the message we have this day. My name is Anka. Father Jozo speaks only Croatian and I will serve as his English interpreter... Father Jozo."

As soon as Fr. Jozo began to speak, I could sense something very special about him. Even though he was speaking through his interpreter, I felt I was hearing everything directly from him. He had a strong and steady voice but he spoke with sincerity and softness. His voice drew me in like he had something very important to say to all of us, and I wanted to make sure I didn't miss a word. As he told the story of the early days when the children first saw the Virgin Mary, there was nothing sensational or overly animated in his expression. There was a quiet conviction and confidence with which he spoke and, while he was very warm and patient in his delivery, there was also seriousness, almost a plea for us to really listen to what he was saying. I felt like he spoke with the authority of heaven and every word mattered. I sensed that I was in the presence of something holy and that his words came from the Holy Spirit. We could have heard a pin drop, even with all the people in attendance. I had been to many church services and I had felt words speak to my heart before but this was like listening to one of the original disciples tell you a story about what they had witnessed themselves in the presence of Jesus. I sensed a holiness I had never really experienced before. Even though he did not speak English, I had the strangest feeling that after a few minutes I was no longer listening to his translator.

Fr. Jozo told us the story of the first days and how he was bewildered, not knowing what he should do. As the priest in charge of the Medjugorje parish he felt a tremendous responsibility and knew he needed to handle the events that were occurring with tremendous care and caution. At first he didn't believe the children at all and he questioned them severely, trying to see if anyone was putting them up to this. He was concerned because so many people were coming to Medjugorje and following the children up the hill, instead of attending church. He worried that in the end it would prove to be a hoax and be used to discredit the faith. He had prayed earnestly to God in distress, asking Him what he should do. As he was praying alone in his church, God spoke to him and gave him the answer, "Go out and protect the children." From that moment on, he began to believe.

Fr. Jozo also talked about the importance of prayer, especially prayer in the family. He talked to us about our material wealth in the West and that faith and hope and love were missing. He also spoke of the sanctity of marriage and how one of Satan's primary goals was to destroy marriage and shake the foundations of the family. He told us that when young couples came to him seeking to be married, he would ask each of them to bring a stick. In his counseling of the couple, he would ask them to tie the two sticks together in the form of a cross, with twine or yarn. He would then tell them not to ever come asking for a divorce unless they could tear the cross they had made apart. That was a message that has *stayed with me forever and, whenever Don and I would hit a hard spot in our marriage, I would always remember this.*

Fr. Jozo went on to talk to us about the Bible story of David and Goliath, explaining that David had trusted only in God's help and the five stones that the Lord had told him to gather. Even though he was just a young boy, he had been able to defeat and kill Goliath who was a strong giant everyone feared. This story was used to compare and to illustrate the five main messages that the Virgin Mary is giving the world and her primary reason for coming to Medjugorje. Her purpose here is to guide our lost world back to her son, Jesus. To help us she has also given us five important stones. These stones are given to help us overcome our weaknesses and to guide us into a life of conversion and a deeper relationship with her Son. The five stones that Mary gives us are Prayer, Fasting, the Eucharist, the Bible and Confession. She tells us that using these stones will help us develop our spiritual potentials.

The first stone we are given is prayer. The most frequent messages from Mary in Medjugorje are about the importance of prayer. She insists that without prayer we cannot truly know God. She reminds us that God grants special graces when we pray and that we are to pray sincerely with our hearts, like little children. She also recommends that we pray the Rosary, telling us that it is a strong prayer against the powers of Satan.

The second stone we have is Fasting. Fasting is offering a sacrifice to God, not just with our prayers but with our whole being. Fr. Jozo told us that through fasting we can defeat our egos, become capable of understanding our neighbors and learn how to love others more. Through fasting we are better able to hear God and man and to see our circumstances more clearly. When asked, Mary recommended that we fast on Wednesdays and Fridays with bread and water.

The third stone is the Eucharist. Fr. Jozo talked about the mystery and the gift of the bread (the body) and wine (the blood) of Jesus and how it transforms and sanctifies us. In her messages, Mary tells us that we do not comprehend the importance of the Eucharist and during one of the apparitions she cried, saying that too many people do not have enough respect for the Eucharist and they do not prepare themselves properly before receiving this gift.

The fourth stone we are given is the Bible. Fr. Jozo talked about how the Bible was born out of the heart of the Lord and that it is His Word to us and should be compared to no other book on earth. Mary asked that we read the Bible every day in our homes and to put it in a visible place to encourage us to read and pray. She also asked that this holy book be placed in a separate place from other books on a shelf.

Confession is the fifth stone we have been given. Fr. Jozo said that confession is not something that you do out of habit, nor is it for the purpose of simply recounting your sins. He said that, instead, it is a beautiful sacrament and a coming to peace with oneself in a meeting with the Lord. In confession, we receive the forgiveness and peace from the Lord so that we can in turn forgive and have peace with others. In one of her messages, Mary had said that the Western Church has disregarded the importance of confession and that monthly confessions would help remedy some of the problems in the West. Father Jozo spoke to us about many more things, but as he concluded his message, he bowed his head in prayer and left the altar through the door he had entered. Near the front of the church, a spontaneous song broke out that began spreading throughout the church. In just a few minutes, Fr. Jozo unexpectedly re-entered the church and walked over to speak to his interpreter. He whispered into her ear and you could see her nod her head in agreement. They talked another second or two and she held up her hands to get everyone's attention as the song people were singing was about to end. Fr. Jozo stepped back to allow her to speak for him. She picked up the microphone and said, "Father Jozo has been given a message that he is to pray for each of you individually. This has happened before but it is very unusual and special graces have always been given. There is a very large crowd here today so it is necessary that you follow my instructions so we can accomplish this in an orderly fashion. Father Jozo has asked each of you, if you would like, to come and stand here at the front of the altar so that he might pray for you. We will start with those that are seated in the aisles first, so that the ones in the pews will be able to move more freely."

There was an immediate sense of excitement in the room as those in the center aisles began to stand and move forward to line up at the altar about thirty to forty people across. Don leaned over to me and whispered, "Do you realize how long this is going to take? We'll be here all day." I ignored the comment and continued watching as Fr. Jozo moved down to the left side of the church. When he came down, he stood about two or three feet in front of the first person. As soon as everyone in the first row had lined up, Fr. Jozo bowed his head to pray and he began walking past each person with his right hand raised toward them. As he began to walk past people with his head bowed many started to fall backwards and the people standing behind them had to catch them to keep them from hitting the stone floor. I didn't know what to think. I was witnessing something I had never witnessed before, except maybe a few times on TV when a loud preacher was yelling, "Be healed," or something else. Looking at that, I thought it was strange and maybe they were getting a little help with a push. I wasn't sure how I felt about those kinds of displays. This was very different. This was quiet, peaceful and felt very holy. Fr. Jozo did not even place his hands on the people standing there. He simply walked by in silent prayer with his right hand held up and they were falling. I was struck with both awe and fear, but nevertheless, I was compelled and wanted to go down to be blessed.

DON

I was witnessing something so unfamiliar to me, but I was immediately struck by two certainties. Number one, this was incredible and number two, there was no way I was going down there! While Fr. Jozo's message had been very moving and had helped me ease some of the bitter emotions I had been feeling on the bus ride over, I still felt like this wasn't for me. This was for those people of God who seemed to have been chosen and who somehow had offered themselves freely to receive Him. There was something about them that was different. Whatever was going on, I was sure it wasn't for someone like me who had become so resistant. Somewhere in the back of my mind I'm sure I didn't want to go down and have another Billy Graham experience. I turned to look at Judy to see what she was thinking and she had a look of amazement at what she was witnessing. In another minute, I turned back to her again and asked, "Are you going down there?" She looked at me and nodded her head yes. "Why am I not surprised?" I thought to myself, "Of course, she's going." Judy's answers were always yes. Just like when I asked her if she was going to go to Medjugorje. There was no, "Well, I'm thinking about it" or "I don't know, what do you think" it was "yes" without hesitation. Judy then turned to me and asked "Are you going?" I answered, "No, no way." As all of this was occurring, people began singing spontaneously and as one song would end, someone would start another song. The music was assisted by one lone guitarist. It appeared to be the same guy that had joined us our first evening, when we had walked to the Blue Cross at the bottom of Apparition Hill. It was beautiful to hear all these voices mixed together singing *Ava Maria* and *Hallelujah* in this beautiful hall. Judy and I continued to watch in silence, until it was getting closer and closer to time for those sitting in our row to go down.

I had made up my mind that I was going to stay back and wait for Judy in the back of the church when she turned to me again and said, "Go with me". Somehow, I was waiting on that but I still shook my head, "no." She waited a few minutes and again turned to me and said, "Please, just go down with me." It was hard to resist her because, in a way, I felt like she was asking me to go "for her" and not just "with" her. I thought I might have picked up on a little uncertainty in her too. With some hesitation, I agreed to go but I told her emphatically, "That's not going to happen to me." Judy replied, "I don't care. I just want to go together." When the time arrived for us to go forward, I reluctantly followed Judy out of the pew. I had some time to think on the way down to the altar and I decided this would be a good opportunity for us to receive a blessing for our marriage. With this thought in my mind, I reached for Judy's hand and we continued holding hands as we lined up in front of the altar.

> For he was a good man, filled with
> the Holy Spirit and faith. And a large
> number of people were
> added to the Lord.

> Acts 11:24
> The New American Bible

Chapter 13

Blinded by the Light

DON

We were standing facing the altar, still holding hands. I was on Judy's left as Fr. Jozo began to move toward us from my left. Fr. Jozo was only slightly shorter than me, and as he approached me, you could see the intense prayer coming from him. I watched as he continued past me without incidence. Just as quickly, he stopped and turned to face Judy, and placed both of his hands on her head. I watched him as he prayed over her for a few moments. When he had finished praying with Judy he looked at her silently and then for some reason he decided to do something that I had not observed him do before: he turned back and looked at me placing one of his hands on my head as he bowed his head in prayer. At that instant, it was as if the room exploded into a brilliant blinding white light and I could not see anything. The last thing I saw was Fr. Jozo's two dark eyes. With the explosion of light I felt my spirit jump inside me. The light began to swirl about in front of me in bands of white light and darkness, just like the aerial view of a hurricane on a radar screen. In the center of this whirling light there were still the two dark dots, but they had now transitioned and moved some distance far away from me. They appeared now to be across the room. It was then that I first realized these were no longer Fr. Jozo's eyes but instead, they now appeared to be more like portholes. I had a strong desire to see what lay beyond them. I also had the understanding that through these portholes was the path to all the knowledge of the universe's existence. In a moment, the portholes began to move back toward me and out of these swirling lights, an image began to take shape in black and white. Slowly, I began to see the face of a man emerge like it was coming out of a fog and these portholes had become his eyes. His face moved toward me from out of the storm. The look on this face was nothing like anything I had ever observed on the face of any man. A countenance was on his face unlike anything I had ever experienced before. It was dirty and bruised. Around his head was a crown of dark black thorns pressed into his head. This was the face of a man that was heavy with the sin of everyone there. Looking at His face caused me deep pain and made me want to cry as I began to see the reflection of my own sin upon His face. Understanding that my sins were also being reflected in His stricken face sickened me and it began to be more than I could endure. At this moment I felt His tremendous love and compassion, as well as the understanding that He knew I could bear no more. Immediately, there was another explosion of light and another hurricane, but this time the colors were red and orange and the light was pulsating. Behind Him was a rainbow of beautiful light. My eyes felt like they were blinking in rhythm with the pulsations. I then began to see the face in full color and noticed His eyes were the deepest blue imaginable. He had high cheek bones, a thin face, a narrow nose and very long, black curly hair and a black beard. Even though the curls were tight, His hair looked like silk and had a beautiful sheen to it and it seemed that you could run your hands thought it without ever finding a tangle. For a brief moment, it appeared like there was still blood on His face from the thorns. Then again, in a moment, His countenance changed and the agony on His face was gone. Instead, His face was alive with intensity and a purpose and undisputable authority. Looking at His face, there was a flood of deep love and companionship that flowed from Him and washed all over me. This person was not a stranger to me. There was an incredible sense that I knew Him well and

He had known me for a long time and was my best friend. It felt like my spirit leaped forward, out of my body, in a rush to meet Him. At the same time my body began to fall. In the middle of this I began to experience an unbelievable peace that had no explanation. In His presence there was an intense feeling of love. I felt only acceptance and there was no condemnation coming from Him.

I had neither confusion nor a need to say or ask anything. All I felt was complete serenity and total surrender. I had no will or any fear to resist what was happening to me. I was blind to anything around me except what was taking place immediately before me. His presence was so real that I wanted to reach out and touch him but I could not move my arms. At the same time, I was not totally unaware of my surroundings. I knew that I was falling and was aware that there was a man standing behind me trying to catch me but he had fallen too and I had fallen on top of him. Although I had some sense of what was going on with my physical body, I had no will to resist and so I obediently yielded as my body went limp and peacefully fell backwards. As I fell, my field of vision grew and I began to see the full torso of the man. I instantly recognized that it was Jesus who stood before me. I didn't know this because he looked like a picture I had seen. In fact, He did not resemble any images I was familiar with. I knew this because my spirit knew it and there was a familiarity like we had met before and he knew everything about me. As his full body came into view from head to toe, I saw his right hand, which was held out at waist height. He moved his fingers only slightly outward toward me from his waist and that was the moment that I began to fall. It was as if he commanded me to fall with his hand. His garments were unfamiliar to me. He was clothed in a black robe with a red undergarment and he wore a reddish orange sash around his waist. Something about this clothing carried with it the impression of raiment of the highest authority. As He began to speak, I had no power to move. All I felt was intense peace and pleasure just because I was in His presence. Then He spoke my name, which gave me joy like I had never felt before. He began to speak, "Don, you are mine. I've claimed you from the beginning of time. This is the true meaning of the vision this morning. We stand apart on two different shores because you have separated your-self from me. The waves that were moving back and forth between you and me represent your faith as you have, at times, moved toward me and other times moved away. The ocean of water does not represent your sin; rather, it is My eternal water. I have enough water to wash away your sins and the sins of the world. I have infinite forgiveness and capacity for love." Then He said, "Help Me Don, don't hurt me!" I had a hard time comprehending this. I have never had a sense that I could ever do anything to help God. He was all powerful and needed no one's help. Yet He invited me and included me in His kingdom as a partner. He continued His message to me..."I need you to be as a good soldier. When you help me you're freeing me to help others. The more you help me, the closer you come to me and the more you will be trusted and the more you will know. There will come a time when all things will be revealed, but for now you do not have the capacity to understand." He also had a general message for people who traveled to Medjugorje. He said that, "All people are called here and they come looking for a gift or an answer to a prayer. Too often, they confine this gift to what they think they need from me. If they will open their hearts to receive what I will give them, it will be the gift they need and the desire of their hearts." He also gave me specific messages for certain people in our group, which I later delivered and after I delivered these messages I could no longer recall the details. He told me, "They know what they want, but I know what they need. If they will accept the gift I give, it will truly be the best gift. Judy misses her mother, but I know the gift she really desires." He then told me what this special gift would be.

Then He acknowledged questions that had haunted me and He left me completely satisfied in His answers. After I had received many messages, I was then given a different kind of vision. Jesus was no longer standing in front of me and I had a sense of being high above him and looking down on Him as He guided me through this vision. I then saw Him walking through a large city, with many tall buildings, similar to New York City, and the buildings fell to the ground as He walked by. My first impression was that it was as though nothing in the universe had power over Him. Not me, not giant buildings, or anything made of man could stand in His presence. His dominion was unquestionable. I had a true sense that He comprised all the power in the Universe. I believe this is true, however, reflecting upon this years later, I felt that I had possibly missed the total message and that He was guiding me through a scene that was to happen sometime in the future.

My vision then moved to another scene. The two scenes seemed to be connected in some way beyond my understanding. In this scene, He stood as an Admiral on the bridge of a war ship and there was a fleet of warships surrounding Him. All He needed to do was to look at the other ships and they would do His will. The ships were sailing from west to east. These were modern day destroyers- grey in color. The feeling was that I was witnessing a vision of some future event but I did not understand what or when at this time. He possessed an intensity that commanded not only the deepest respect but also the intentness of purpose.

The visions and this information was being passed to me at such a rapid speed that I felt like I was a hard drive on a computer. The information was coming in so fast I could not process it immediately. I had a sense it would take me years to process everything. During the entire time my body felt levitated and pulsating in His presence.

In a while, I began to hear another voice calling to me. It was Judy. She was softly trying to speak to me. "Don, Don, are you all right?" I could not answer her. It was as though I was slowly coming out of anesthesia. I realized I was beginning to regain control of my body again. I lay on the stone floor for another minute or two and I slowly began to regain my senses and my sight. As I began to regain my sight, my eyes felt like they were blinking rapidly. I then realized the gentleman I had fallen on had somehow removed himself but I had no idea of how or when. The first thing I saw was Judy kneeling over me and I could see she had tears running down her cheeks. In a few moments Judy and another man helped me to my feet. Judy took my hands, to steady me, and we found our way back to where we had been sitting.

JUDY

When Fr. Jozo came to me, I was stunned that he had paused and placed both of his hands on my head and then gone back to Don. I can only assume it was the Holy Spirit that led him to do this, but it is something I will always be curious about. When he did this and Don fell, I was amazed and I had no idea what I should do so I just stood there for a while looking down at him. It was obvious something was happening to him. His eyes were closed but you could see that under his eye lids they were moving back and forth rapidly, as if he was watching something moving in front of him. He stayed there like this for a good while and I continued to just stand there and watch. In a while, others who had fallen were getting up and I kneeled down to touch Don's arm but Don did not respond. I waited a few more minutes and then I began to try to speak to him. Once I did this, he slowly began to open his eyes and, with the help of another man, he stood up. When we got back to our seats, Don sat down quietly, on the edge of the pew, with his head bowed down between his hands. I knew from the expression on his face that something had happened to him and I instinctively knew to leave him alone. At one point, I placed my hand on his back and he just turned and looked at me, shaking his head, as if he couldn't speak. Don turned away and bowed his head again and then he began to sob, loudly, like I have never heard him or anyone else sob before. These were not quiet tears and they sounded like tears he had been holding back for years. You could hear him sobbing from the depths of his soul, all over the church. I still cry to this day when I think about it. I just put my arms around him, without saying a word, and felt him release a lifetime of tears. At some point, someone had handed me some tissue and when Don had finished crying, I gave it to him. In a few minutes, he had regained his composure and turned to me, still shaking his head in astonishment at what had happened to him and said, "Judy, I think I just saw Christ". At this point, I think his mind simply could not comprehend what he knew he had just seen. We sat there with my arms around him for a while. The church had almost emptied out when someone from our group came in to see if we were ready to leave.

By this time, most of the people in our group had already gotten on the bus and had been patiently waiting on us. It was obvious to everyone something very personal had happened to Don and everyone was very respectful to leave us alone to ourselves on the ride back. Don did not share anything more with me on the 40 minute ride home. On the bus ride over he had been agitated and quite vocal about everything that was irritating him. He was hot under the collar and sweating in the 100 plus temperature. At this particular moment, he was quiet and in deep thought. Oddly, he was also shivering as if it was cold outside.

DON

The bus trip back to Medjugorje was a blur to me. I was still caught up in a narcosis, trying to recover my senses. My mind was on complete overload as to what I had just witnessed, and the experience left me numb. It was as if everything in my world had been turned on its axis. North was no longer North anymore. My mind was spinning and searching for meaning. The heat of the afternoon went unnoticed as my mind was consumed by what had happened. In fact, I felt a chill. I began to understand everything that had happened to me was a part of the whole. It had started with Sister Delores, when she shared her vision and asked me to pray so Jesus would reveal what it meant. The vision I had of Judy's mother was something I had never experienced before but it was just a small introduction to what I had encountered at the church. Listening to Fr. Jozo speak about a life of conversion and his honesty about his own doubts had encouraged me and opened my mind to a bigger picture of what was happening here. Seeing Jesus and hearing him call me by my name and tell me He had claimed me since the beginning of time, broke through every pain or feeling of rejection. He brought with Him such peace, acceptance and clarity. He cut through to the core of everything and exposed the lies I had been told, by the enemy of my soul, on the floor at Billy Graham's Crusade. He made it clear He accepted me and showed me His uncompromising love and forgiveness without an ounce of condemnation towards me. His words kept echoing in my ear. "If people will accept the gifts I give them it will reach the core of what their heart truly desires."

I came here thinking I needed nothing, yet Jesus knew better. He knew about my emptiness and the sadness and the feelings of rejection. He understood my confusion and the anger I had stored up for a long time. In almost an instance and with one look, He had flushed all of that out. Even more so, He had recruited me into His army and had asked me to stop hurting Him and to become a good soldier. He was gentle and kind but also mighty and strong and everything He did and said had such purpose. There was no wasted effort in Him. He told me He would one day answer all my questions and gave me a promise that I would grow in understanding. He said He had known me since the beginning of time. He was the good shepherd that left His flock to go find His one lost sheep. At the moment, that lost sheep had been me. As I continued to look out the window, deep in my thoughts, it gripped me that I could have missed this. Now I realize it was no accident that Judy came into my life. We had not begun our relationship with the greatest purity but God was working on both of us. That thought hit me like a brick- "The both of us." No longer was

I feeling like the uninvited outsider or someone who had just tagged along because of Judy's calling. No longer did Judy's faith frighten me. Instead it bonded me to her more and gave greater meaning to our marriage and my love for her. I had never known such amazing love or acceptance and it took the sting out of everything that had gone on before. While I still had much to process regarding my vision, on this matter I was now certain. Yes, now I know that it was no accident that Judy came into my life.

After we returned and had dinner, Judy and I called it an early evening. When we were in our room, we laid down on the bed and held each other and I began to tell her everything. When I finished, Judy turned to me and said, "Don, it feels like there are angels in our room right now." This is when I realized my gift was not over. In that moment, God again lifted the veil from my eyes and I could see what Judy perceived, only I had to tell her we were surrounded by angels. There was a tall angel standing in the corner of the room. He was bald and had on a long, white robe. This angel was reading from an open book that he held outward in both hands. I couldn't hear him but his lips were moving and I really wanted to know what he was reading. I felt like he was reading something written long ago and he was releasing words that involved me. Around his head and covering the entire ceiling were small cherub angels looking down on us and hugging each other. More startling, and of some concern to me, was the presence of a war-like arch-angel. He was standing outside our room on the window ledge. He was very large and was a bronze color and in his right hand was a huge golden sword laying across his chest. He was not looking at us but instead he was gazing out, in a true sentinel 1000-yard gaze. I immediately knew he was there to protect the angel reading the book, as well as Judy and me. I felt totally safe. I began to realize the battles that go on for the souls of men, and Jesus had just made His enemy furious. My belief is that Satan was confident he had me in his trap of lies and now that he had lost that battle he wanted to attack me again. He thought he had me, but now I knew that at no time was I ever out of the watchful eye of God. Satan must have been angry because this archangel was seriously protecting us.

Our discussion went on into the night about what I should do with this. Should I share what had happened with the others at breakfast or keep this to myself? I wondered what the others would think. Out of everyone on our trip, I would be the last person anyone would expect to receive such a gift. Almost everyone knew I had not wanted to come. They had been very respectful and had given me my space earlier this evening but I was sure there would be questions in the morning.

All of this had been extremely taxing on me and I still didn't know what to do with my experience. I looked again at the angel standing on the ledge. The expression on his face was both comforting and frightening. I knew that, whatever was out there, I was glad to have this angel on my side. I felt it was important to write down the things that Christ had said so I began writing a journal of what I heard, what I saw and what I felt. I think I finally nodded off in the middle of a thought while Judy was still sitting up and listening to me.

> For God did not send His Son into
> the world to condemn the world,
> but that the world might be
> saved through Him.

John 3:17
The New American Bible

Chapter 14

The Sharing

JUDY

There is no way to describe what I felt as Don told me what he had experienced at Fr. Jozo's church. After talking for some time, we laid there holding each other and I felt the presence of something in our room. I had not seen anything with my eyes but I distinctly felt there were angels in our room. My sense was that they were small and they were high in the room. I could also sense their joy and pleasure looking down at us. I turned to Don and quietly whispered to him that I thought there were angels in the room. Don had seemed pleasantly amused when he said, "Judy, the room is full of angels." Sometimes I think God gives you the grace to believe because, just like when Terri had given me the message that day in my office, I had no problem believing Don now either. I could feel their presence and at that moment I felt an indescrib-

able peace and an overwhelming sense of love and joy. Don and I stayed up late into the night talking about everything that had happened. Now, this morning, Don still seemed very much at peace. He looked as if he was fifty pounds lighter. Like a load had been lifted off of him. Everything about him was calm. He was patient while waiting on me to get ready and his tone was softer. The effects of the previous day were still with him and his face even looked different to me.

We made our way downstairs to find almost everyone already there waiting for breakfast at the dining room table. Everyone's mood seemed bright and people were chatting and laughing with each other like you might imagine the morning after an exciting event where everyone was talking about how much fun they had the day before. Only this wasn't happening after the big football game, or concert, or exciting presidential election. This was the morning after an incredible church service, where the real presence of God had been felt by so many. People's hearts had been lifted and lives had been changed forever. Toward the end of breakfast, everyone started sharing things they had felt or witnessed during Fr. Jozo's talk and eventually someone asked Don if he felt he could share with the group what had happened to him. Almost everyone knew that something had happened to Don. Some had been nearby and had witnessed him fall. Others had heard his deep cry while in the church. Everyone had patiently waited on the bus for us to eventually come out of the church. I knew they had noticed how quiet we both were on the ride home and how close we had stuck together. Everyone had been so thoughtful the night before sensing Don wasn't able to talk about it.

This morning they were ready to hear and several people joined in to encourage Don to share with them what had happened. Before Don began to share his story, he felt it was important for those who did not know him well to first understand a little about him. He began by explaining how he had resisted coming to Medjugorje. He continued to share that after getting to the church and listening to Fr. Jozo he had been very moved by his message. At some point, Fr. Jozo had talked about John the Baptist and Don told the group that, out of all the characters in the Bible, he had always identified with John the most. Don described John the Baptist as someone who had gone out alone, into the wilderness, determined to accomplish his mission. John had no problem telling you the truth as he saw it, even if you were royalty. I immediately began to understand why Don related to John the Baptist so much. I wasn't sure Don was giving a full portrayal of John the Baptist but as he was describing him I knew in many ways he was also describing himself. Don had always been that lone wolf and he seemed quite content to be that way. He didn't seem to need the company of others and he would most often go off on his own to do something by himself. Also, Don never had a problem letting others know what he thought of them if he felt there was a need to do it. Just like John the Baptist he would "call people out." This had caused him problems from time to time, just like John the Baptist. Fortunately, I thought, it had not cost him his head yet but I knew it had indeed cost him at times. As he was talking about this, someone made the comment that we need to call you "Don, the Batholic," referring to his Baptist upbringing here in this very Catholic setting. This brought the house down with laughter.

Don went on to explain that he was baptized as a teenager but he had drifted away as he had gotten older. He had lived a pretty selfish life focused on himself and his work always thinking he was the one in charge of everything. He continued to share many other things about his past leading up to what had happened to him four years earlier. I listened intently as he began to relate what had happened to him that night on the floor of the Billy Graham Crusade. My thoughts drifted back to that night. I listened to him share how he had felt a call in his spirit to go down after the service only to be overcome with a terrible, sickening sense of unworthiness and a feeling that he had not been wanted by God. I remembered that night well. I had always known that something had happened when Don came back up from the floor and sat back down. He had seemed disturbed and he wanted us to leave immediately. Someone behind us must have noticed too because on the way out this young man came up to Don and asked him if he could pray for him. Don had seemed a little embarrassed but had told him it was O.K. He finished praying, I thanked him and we walked on out to the car. When we were in the car, I had asked Don what was wrong and he only shook his head and said he didn't want to talk about it. I could tell something was troubling him so I asked him if he would tell me later. He said he would but he had managed to avoid any future questions about that evening. I guess we got busy with life and "later" never came. As I listened to Don tell this story, I couldn't imagine that he had carried these feelings around for all these years. It explained so much and it made me want to cry.

Don had never told anyone about this. He had tried to just push it out of his mind and forget that it ever happened. He explained how, from that point forward, he had really struggled with so many things and that, unfortunately, he had placed his anger on so many that he was close to. This had been the ultimate rejection and he wondered how bad you had to be to be rejected by God. The thought that he had been under a spiritual attack never occurred to him and he had accepted the rejection as real. His anger, hurt, and compounded rejection turned inward and he felt a sense that in this life he had to rely on himself for whatever he needed. I believe the pain and embarrassment of this was so great he would not allow himself to share this with me or anyone else. By not sharing this, he allowed himself to remain in that state of pain. During this time we were not in a Christian community and he had no one to give him a spiritual perspective on what had occurred. This left him in a place of isolation and open to future attacks. Looking back, it is obvious to both of us that not having a community of other Christians to guide us in this was a major mistake that played right into the hands of the enemy. If he had sought some help in community, I am sure that he would have found someone that could have given him a proper perspective of spiritual warfare and how to deal with it.

God did seek to reach out to Don after this but I don't think he was prepared to accept what he heard was from God. He told the group about being upset over a family issue and the voice he had heard in the midst of all of that anger while driving down Live Oak Plantation Road, telling him to, "Give it Up." I remembered that day too. I had driven down that same road at the exact same time to find Don's truck pulled off the side of the road. He could hardly talk as he tried to tell me what had just happened to him. Don shared with us that, when this had happened, it had stopped him in his tracks. He had prayed a simple prayer, asking God to *give him clarity and to take the pain he was carrying away. Don had told me about the voice but not his prayer. I realized that, before coming to Medjugorje, I wasn't sure Don even prayed much more than an occasional blessing at the table. Any suggestion of prayer with me had always been met with resistance. Don shared that after this last incident things had started to get better, especially in his business. He was building more homes than ever and he was selling them even before they were finished. He had to hire more people just to keep up and life seemed to be turning around. All of a sudden, he was feeling like he could do no wrong. We were coming up on our first wedding anniversary and Don was thinking a nice trip back to Bermuda would be a great way to celebrate it all. He was starting to feel really good about things again. As he continued, he said, "That's when you guys came over here and Terri came back saying that the Virgin Mary had given her Judy's name and we were to come back the week before our one year anniversary."*

At this point, Terri jumped in and said, "That's when he told me, 'Terri, I guess you're only going to drink gold light beer now', very sarcastically." There was another large break out of laughter at Terri's comment and Don went on to explain....."Well, that was because you came back talking about your 'thing' turning to gold," meaning her Rosary. Don admitted that he was very sarcastic and had enjoyed teasing

Terri about all of this. His big fear was that he didn't want me to come back home some kind of "hand raising, halle-lujah" Christian.

Don told everyone that once he had gotten to Medjugorje he had become a little more comfortable. After climbing the mountain and seeing the prayers, he began to realize that most of the people here were everyday people who were just seeking a closer relationship with God. He felt he had actually begun to open up a little and he had been looking forward to visiting with the healing nuns and praying for his sister. He told everyone about the nun's vision of him and Christ and his interpretation of what it meant and how this had caused all those feelings of rejection to rush back in. He explained his mood on the bus and why he had not wanted to go hear Fr. Jozo. This also was an explanation of why he did not want to go down and have Fr. Jozo pray for him. He did not want to risk another experience like the one he had had at the Billy Graham Crusade. All of this was to let everyone know who he was and how he had found himself here in Medjugorje.

Once he finished this, he explained more about how he had been moved during Fr. Jozo's talk and exactly what had hap-pened to him when Fr. Jozo had turned back to him. People were silent and there were tears as he revealed his experience.

There were two main messages Don wanted to make sure people received from his vision. One was that each one of us traveling to Medjugorje would receive a gift. Some of us would receive our gift while in Medjugorje but others would not receive their gifts until after they had returned home. He said Christ had said we were not to be jealous of each other's gifts or to feel slighted in the least but instead, we were to be enriched by each other's gifts. The other message was that when we returned home, we should share our gifts with others. He wanted to reaffirm that none of us were here by chance, that we were loved and that God was pleased that we had opened up to Him. Each of us had our own individual gift that we would receive for accepting the invitation to come here.

I could hardly believe this was my husband talking. He spoke with such humility as well as clarity and purpose. He continued telling us that anyone who came to Medjugorje, carrying the kind of pain he had been carrying, needed to know that Jesus cares for them deeply and that He wanted to heal them and set them free from their pain. All they needed to do was to yield to Him to find His forgiveness and they would find more mercy than they could ever imagine. Don questioned why he had been given such a gift when he knew there were so many other people, including priests, whom he felt were much more worthy and who had sought God so much more than he had. He explained this by saying that Christ knows what we each need and if we don't receive a *vision we should consider ourselves privileged because Christ knows that it wasn't necessary. He said if we yield to His will, we will receive the most precious gift of all, which is the one we need the most. He emphasized again that many would leave Medjugorje without the gift now because it was not the right time but that we should stay steadfast in the love of Christ and yield to Him and it would come to pass. He went on to say that he had felt no direct condemnation of his sin by Christ. He did feel a deep sense of shame that he had let Christ down. It was then that Christ appealed to him and said, "Help me Don, don't hurt me! Be a good soldier." Christ, instead of condemning him, offered him a position in His Kingdom. Instead of a feeling of rejection, Christ openly accepted Don as one He sought to favor.*

As he was concluding, Henry Desilets spoke up and said something that sounded like a prophesy. "Going forward Don is going to be God's instrument for great things....When Christ moved He moved very rapidly and that's the way that he moved Don...He moved very rapidly so from Don is going to come some great things that He's going to accomplish in Don and your lives. Don may not see them now, but he will see them as the days go by."

When Don finished and sat down, there was a flood gate of others sharing their insights, as well as other experiences they had received over the past few days. It was very moving and I imagined this must have been what it was like in the early days of Christianity, when news began to spread about Jesus and the miracles they had seen Him perform. There was a very strong presence of the Holy Spirit in the room and John Kearney, one of the men in our group, started singing a song of praise. The presence of the Holy Spirit, the intimate sharing and worship in song brought us all even closer together this morning and set a beautiful stage for events that were to follow.

When everyone had concluded talking, Don and I stood up and hugged quietly. There was no need for words. People made their way to Don and hugged him and thanked him for sharing with them. If at any point Don had not felt included or felt there was no reason for him to be here in Medjugorje, I knew this outpouring of love toward him had to have erased all of that. Here Don was embracing all those people he had been so suspicious of in the beginning and more importantly they were embracing him.

DON

Judy and I had discussed the possibility of sharing what had happened to me before we had gone downstairs for breakfast. I had mixed feelings about it. On the one hand, it was very personal, yet there were messages I had been given for members of our group. I think this is what gave me the most apprehension, because I wasn't sure how the messages would be received. I eventually realized this was not up to me and if Jesus had given me this information, it was important. In the end, telling what had happened to me wasn't up to me either. People had started asking questions and I knew this was something I was supposed to share. As I began sharing with everyone at breakfast, I noticed something happening in the room. People were very quiet and paying close attention to every word and some were moved to tears. I wasn't really prepared for this and it was very humbling. The words were mine but the Spirit in the room was God's. I still had my sarcastic wit that brought laughter a time or two, but I felt a new honesty and seriousness that allowed me to deliver words from my heart and it felt amazingly good. All my apprehension had gone and had been replaced by a sense of mission. I had a sense of The Holy Spirit working through me and using me. My words seemed inadequate to explain what I had witnessed or how I felt in the presence of Jesus. Still, I could see that the words were touching everyone's hearts deeply. This gave me a wonderful awareness of being incorporated into God's plan. I was overwhelmed at the gift of love that God had given me and I was completely humbled by the reaction of those in our group. The sense of connection I felt with God and all of his people at this moment was something I had never been able to comprehend before. For the first time I felt completely free from my feelings of separation and isolation.

After breakfast Judy looked at me and squeezed my hand and I knew I had made her happy. I had either surprised her speechless or maybe I was finally becoming the guy that she had always believed in.

How good and pleasant it is when
God's people live together in unity!

Psalm 133:1
New International Version

Chapter 15

The Angels

JUDY

After experiencing the wonderful sharing during breakfast the only things we had on our schedule for the remainder of the day was a Mass and a later visit to Vicka Ivankovic's house. Vicka was another one of the visionaries who was sixteen years old when the apparitions began. Vicka's house was located across several fields from St. James, near the foot of Apparition Hill. We wanted to get to her home early in order to get close enough to hear everything she had to say. Listening to these Seers, who were now in their mid to late twenties, was like receiving manna from Heaven. They spoke beautifully, with such simplicity and sincerity. Listening to the words they had received from the Virgin Mary, about God's love for mankind and His call for the world to turn back to Him, was like an elixir for the soul.

I knew there would be many people who would have a difficult time believing this was actually happening. I wished they could all be here where they could listen to the messages these young people were sharing with the world. I believed if anyone could hear the words coming out of their mouths they would know these were messages from the heart of Mary calling people back to her son, Jesus.

I had been taught the Bible as a young person and I knew what it said about testing the spirits. One of the first things to test was whether the spirit professed that Jesus had come in the flesh. Without a question, Mary professed that Jesus had come in the flesh; he had died and had risen. The other way to test a spirit was to see if it followed the teachings of the apostles. I had not found anything in Mary's messages that contradicted scripture. In fact, during the first three months someone had asked the children to ask the Virgin Mary if there were other intermediaries, besides Jesus, between God and Man. She answered by saying, "There is only one mediator between God and man, and it is Jesus Christ". That response answered a lot of people's questions, especially those who found fault with those in the Catholic faith saying that they prayed to Mary. I was beginning to unravel this for myself and had come to understand that it was more that they asked her to pray for and with them. "Holy Mary, pray for us, now and at the hour of our death" was part of the Rosary prayer that we had come to know. I, for one, felt I could use all the prayers in the world including those from the Saints who had gone on before. It was not that big of a stretch for me to believe that all the Saints in Heaven would be pulling for each of us down here still struggling on earth and I felt sure they must pray. All my inner conflicts, regarding the Rosary and Mary, had been put at ease. This place was beautiful. The messages were of God's love and the fruits of God's love were present everywhere. People were turning back to God, confessing their sins, turning to prayer and reading their Bibles. People were going to church and participating in communion. Prayers were being answered and people were being healed. Many graces were being handed out here and the faith of the people was evident.

When we arrived at Vicka's house, a crowd had already gathered. We tried to get up as close as we could and as we pressed forward there was a shift in the crowd and Terri and I moved to the right with the crowd. I tried to motion to Don to let him know where we were going but the crowd was too thick for him to make his way to us. He shouted to me that if we got separated he would meet us at the Church. In a few moments Vicka came out of her home and stood on an outside staircase above the crowd along with an interpreter. A lot of the questions were similar to the kinds of questions people had asked Ivan earlier in the week. Just like with Ivan, I was so impressed with the poise and grace that she exhibited here day after day. Vicka just beamed when she talked about the Virgin Mary. She spoke with such joy and love and she wore a beautiful smile the entire time she talked to us. She had a child-like innocent joy when she talked and you would never know that she stood here several times a week, telling the same story to a new group of pilgrims. After about 40 minutes of answering everyone's questions, Vicka waved and then turned to go back into her house and the crowd began to break up. I had lost sight of Don and after waiting a few minutes, Terri and I decided to head on back to the church in order to make it to the noon Mass.

DON

When Judy and I were separated by the crowd I wasn't concerned because I knew it would be easy to catch up with her later. While listening to Vicka this morning, the words were more alive than ever to me. Her words were not beyond my comprehension any more - neither was her joy.

After the crowd began to disperse, I waited to see if I could find Judy and Terri but they were nowhere to be seen. It was as if they had disappeared into thin air. Over the crowd, I had yelled for Judy to meet me at the church and I was hoping she had heard me. I knew she and Terri had planned on going to Mass, so I decided to head on back and try to meet them at the end of the orchard, since this is the route we had taken on the way over. This seemed to be the most direct path back to the church and all I had to do was follow a wide clay path through the fields.

The clay path with Apparition Hill in background

St. James, with its two large towers, was easily visible straight ahead. Walking back, I felt exhilarated. It was a beautiful morning and there was a momentary break in the heat. I was having one of those moments you have when all of your senses are wide awake and you are just glad to be alive. The sensory overload I had experienced the day before had calmed down and now I was left with the simple truth of God's love. I was taking everything in this morning, like I was breathing and seeing and tasting everything for the first time. Here I was, walking on a clay path through vineyards in a remote village somewhere on a map in Yugoslavia. Tobacco fields and sheep were on my right as I passed three peasant ladies, dressed in dark dress, who had set up a make-shift shop on the edge of the path under a tree. One lady was hand spinning wool onto a large spool. Another woman was crocheting small items and the third woman had their goods spread out on several blankets offering them for sale. As I moved on past them, I smiled and headed on toward the church that lay ahead in the distance.

Looking around I realized I was completely alone on this path through the vineyards. All of a sudden I felt the ground shake; it stopped me in my tracks. After the small earthquake we had experienced earlier, I assumed that's what this was. I stood there for a few seconds with my feet braced shoulder width apart waiting to see if it was going to happen again. Nothing more happened so, feeling secure, I took two more steps forwards. Again the ground shook all around me, but this time there was something new that came with it. It sounded like hundreds of people were coming up behind me. I took another step and heard this rumble akin to a fleet of tanks moving up behind me. I quickly turned 180° to see if a crowd of people were rushing across the field towards me. Turning around the breath went out of me. I was stunned and I would have fallen to my knees, if I could have moved. Suddenly before me there stood a massive army of angels, by the thousands, maybe millions. They were coming down from Heaven in a picture-like cornucopia stretching up into Heaven and disappearing out of sight over Apparition Hill. The widest part of the army was closest to me with the narrowest part diminishing far away from me over the hill. The formation of this army of angels was unlike any army I had ever seen on a march before. They were marching in rows stacked on top of rows seven tiers high. I don't have the words to describe how magnificent they were. They had flags and bugles and we stood with eyes on each other, like gunslingers in a face-off. They did not move any further forward once I had turned around towards them. I just stood there looking at them as they looked at me. Their flags waived in a gentle breeze and I instinctively thought they were waiting for me to move. I didn't know how, or why, or when I did this but I eventually turned and took a few steps towards St. James. The rumble moved again. I quickly spun around to face them still disbelieving what my eyes were seeing. They were still there just standing with their flags waiving. Again I moved forward and again the same pattern was repeated. I would move and they would begin to move. I would stop and they would stop. To this day I will never know how I finally proceeded on to St. James but something just told me I needed to go on.

God had to have allowed me to see this splendid sight for a reason. I later reflected upon this and I believe that God wanted me to know that we are not alone and that when we are asked to be a good soldier in His army, we can go forward confidently in knowing who and what is behind us. I went on to St. James after this and met Judy for Mass. During the Mass, I contemplated everything I had witnessed, although I did not share this with Judy immediately. I knew she would have many questions. At the moment I was having a hard enough time, by myself, trying to process and understand the meaning of what was being revealed to me.

JUDY

After the Noon Mass, I was glad we had some free time to just walk around the village and mingle with the locals. At the time we were in Medjugorje, there were only a handful of small shops that had sprung up to cater to all those traveling there. We decided to visit a few after a quick lunch. The only things these shops carried were religious objects such as Rosaries, medals, prayer cards, crosses or crucifixes. Don and I headed out to see if there was anything we wanted to pick up. We ended up buying a prayer book, a few medals and two more Rosaries, as well as a wall crucifix that I found. Don also bought a gold crucifix. He had been wearing a gold chain with a gold coin around his neck and he replaced the coin with this crucifix. As we were browsing one of the small shops, a local peasant woman walked up to me and handed me a very unique charm. She had incredibly kind eyes but she could not speak English at all. I understood from her head and hand motions that she was giving it to me, as a gift. I reached in my pocket offering to pay her for it but she smiled and shook her head, "No." It was a metal charm that had a cutout of what I assumed was supposed to be the Virgin Mary holding baby Jesus. This particular charm, though, was very different from the traditional rendering of the Virgin Mary. I was used to seeing the Virgin Mary with a long veil and had I not been in Medjugorje I honestly don't think I would have associated this charm with the Virgin Mary at all. The young woman on this charm was not wearing a veil and instead had a scarf on her head much like young girls wear a bandana here in the U.S. The scarf was not tied in front under the chin but in the back underneath the hair so that most of the hair, including the bangs, was showing. I thought it was beautiful and I placed it on my necklace and wore it for years. Even though this charm has no real monetary value, it is extremely meaningful to me and to this day I still keep it in a special place. I later discovered that both Page and Terri had been given this same charm at separate times. This too would become another one of those "coincidences" that would later have meaning to all three of us.

Later in the day, we were all back together again at the dinner table enjoying one of our host's delicious meals. Someone came in to tell us they had learned that one of the visionaries had told a group, earlier that day, there would be an evening apparition on Apparition Hill. Everyone was excited and rushed through dinner to make their way to the hill. Apparition Hill was not nearly as tall as Cross Mountain but it was every bit as treacherous. There were so many people trying to make their way up in the dark, all at the same time. It is hard to imagine that no one was hurt but I think this is another one of the many graces given here. This evening we were going higher up the hill than we had on our first night here. We moved as close to the site as we could, but there were a lot of people between us and the vision-aries. Someone began to lead the crowd in praying a Rosary. I remember looking across toward Cross Mountain and I could barely see the Cross from this distance, as the sun had now set. All I could see was a hint of light near the horizon. Additionally, I could see flickering lights from candles that had been lit at the base of the cross. About halfway through the Rosary, we heard a hush rush over the crowd from the direction of the visionaries, signifying that the Virgin Mary was present. There was complete silence for at least 15 minutes. It was hard to imagine the Virgin Mary could be just a few yards away, yet it was possible. Otherwise, how could all of this be explained?

There had been other apparitions of Mary recorded throughout history. Some of the most well known had been in Fatima and Lourdes. She had always brought messages of hope as well as warnings important for those times. Here she was in Medjugorje, asking for people to convert and turn to God. The visionaries said Mary told them that she would not appear on earth again the way she was doing, now, in Medjugorje. She said this was a special time of grace, given by God, and that she was preparing for her Son to come into the world again. She was gently and lovingly asking all people on earth to convert while there was still time. Her messages were always of God's love but there was also seriousness in them. According to the visionaries Mary has told them that a time of darkness has come upon the earth as never before. She is here to draw the people of this generation back to the love of God through the truth of Jesus. Most of her messages were to encourage us to pray. She said we could not know God without prayer and that prayer could change the course of our lives and natural events.

Here, in Medjugorje, Mary has given the visionaries secrets that involve global events that will impact the world. They all will receive ten secrets and, to date, three have received all ten and the other three have received nine. The visionaries are often asked to disclose information regarding the secrets but they say very little. They have, however, disclosed that the third secret involves a permanent sign that will appear at the site of the first apparition. We are told the sign will be beautiful and indestructible by man. We are also told that it will be the cause of many more conversions. Instead of being afraid the visionaries tell us to trust God and focus on living a life that is pleasing to Him.

After a while, someone near the visionaries began the Rosary again, letting us know the apparition was over. Once the Rosary was finished, people began singing and turning to make their way back down the mountain. We heard from others that the message would be written down and posted at the church the following day.

Terri, Don and I were standing close together. I saw Don turn to Terri to give her a hug and tell her he had been told by Jesus in his vision what my gift was going to be. Terri asked him if he would tell her and he had told her yes, but made her promise not to tell anyone, especially me. He leaned over and whispered in her ear, and I let it go thinking I would get it out of Terri later on. I was wrong. When I tried to get Terri to tell me she would just look at me, smile and say defiantly, "I'm not going to tell you." I left it alone after a while. There *were too many wonderful things going on here right now. Whatever it was, I was content to wait. We all made it safely down the mountain, headed back to our place and on to bed.*

For God commands the angels to guard you in all your ways.

Psalm 91:11

The New American Bible

Chapter 16

The Feast, Adoration and More

DON

We all woke up this morning with the realization that today would be our last full day in Medjugorje. It was Wednesday, August 15th, and by all indications this was going to be a jam-packed day. The population of Medjugorje was at an all time high, as additional people from the surrounding countries were pouring in to celebrate the Feast Day of the Assumption of Mary. Typically, everyone in Medjugorje would fast on Wednesdays, however today was considered a day of celebration within the Catholic faith so food was in order.

At breakfast, everyone seemed to be in more of a hurry to get out and about to soak in everything they could on this final day of our journey. Some in our group were still hoping they would see a miracle of their own before they left. Others had already experienced some extraordinary miracles. Henry's prayers had been answered and he had seen the "miracle of the sun" the day before. I knew how much he had prayed for this and I was glad to see him so happy. Off and on, I found myself shaking my head at everything that had transpired. I wasn't sure I could handle anything more. I was completely full or at least that is what I thought.

Don and friends in front of St. James, Feast Day morning

A lot of activities had been planned for this Feast Day at St. James so after breakfast we all began to head over to the church courtyard. The main activities were taking place outside in the back courtyard of the church which faced Cross Mountain. On the back side of the church was a large covered outside altar. The church had built this to provide extra space for the additional services needed to accommodate the various languages and the multitude of pilgrims coming from all over the world. There were a few benches in the courtyard but not nearly enough for the number of people that were here today. During the day, it was more of a festival than a church service and people were steadily pouring in and out of the area. From the altar, there was a mixture of singing, priests talking and others giving testimonies about their individual experiences in Medjugorje. Judy and I walked around, with a few others, waiting to see if a place to sit would open up.

We walked around on the east side of the church where there were lines and lines of people waiting to go to confession. At the front of each line was a sign indicating the language of the priest that was hearing confession. It appeared that almost every language was represented: French, German, Portuguese, Italian, Spanish, Polish, English and more. Many of the Catholics in our group had talked about going to confession and I found it humorous as a Protestant to learn that some priests had reputations of being tougher than others. Word somehow got around as to which priests to avoid, if at all possible. For some reason, I had started thinking about going to confession but, being a Protestant, I had never done this and I had no idea how to go about it.

I wasn't sure if it would even be acceptable, since I was not Catholic. For a moment it crossed my mind that maybe it wasn't necessary to tell the priest that I was not Catholic. As soon as that thought entered my mind, I quickly dismissed it. Out of all my many sins, dishonesty was something I despised. In fact, deception had always been difficult for me. Judy often complained that I was honest to a fault, generally referring to times when she would ask me a question like "Do you like this dress?" or "How do you like my new haircut?" I knew myself too well to think I could pull this off, but still I had this strong desire to talk to a priest. To be honest, I didn't want to sit there and review every detail of my sinful life. We were leaving the next day and I was certain I needed more time than we had left to confess all my wrongs. What I really needed was someone who could help me get some spiritual perspectives on everything that had happened to me. Hopefully, I would be able to find a priest with lots of experience and insight. I decided that, before the service this afternoon, I would look among the English speaking priests for an older priest to talk to. For the balance of the morning, we soaked in the sights and sounds of our last day in Medjugorje and took those final photographs.

Although I had not seen the angels again, I was walking around with a second sense that I was never alone. There was an obvious "presence" and I realized that God was with me at all times. It was a wonderful new realization. I felt as though God had poured so much information into me, but I had not been able to process very much of it. It is hard to explain but I think I was in some sort of sensory overload and mild shock at what had happened to me. I had experienced the love of God towards me in a most profound way. At the same time, I couldn't help but wonder what I was supposed to do with everything I had received. I thought surely, if God gives you a wonderful gift you are supposed to do something with it but I was at a complete loss as to what. More importantly, I didn't know for sure if God expected me to do something with it or not. I was walking in new shoes and, although I loved these new shoes, they were not yet comfortable.

It was now getting very hot in the late afternoon and there was no shade to be found anywhere on the back side of the church. The service portion of the day was about to begin and we still had not been able to find a place to sit. We decided to do as thousands of others were doing and kneeled on the hot gravel. I soon learned that this service was not going to be a typical Mass. By now, I thought I had become familiar with almost everything Catholic when I learned there was something I still had not been exposed to: the Eucharistic Adoration Service. This was a solemn service involving songs of praise and adoration, as priests took turns holding up a gold object that looked like a sun burst with a red center. I later learned that this object was called a Monstrance and it held the consecrated host or wafer which is given out during Holy Communion. In the Catholic faith, this is the body of Christ. The purpose of this service was to simply spend time in the presence of Jesus offering Him your thanks, praise and love.

Judy and I positioned ourselves fairly close to the front near the altar. The heat was bearing down on us and the sun was low in the sky but still very bright. I was really glad I had my sunglasses with me. They were designed for snow skiing and they wrapped all the way around my eyes to keep the wind as well as the glare out. They were great for helping your vision but because they were mirrored no one could see your eyes through the lens.

The glasses were doing a great job of keeping the sun out of my eyes but the gravel under my knees was making things very uncomfortable. I found myself in deep thought, reflecting on all that had happened to us during the week and I realized as my mind was wandering that I was not paying a lot of attention. I pulled myself away from my thoughts and back to this unfamiliar service. After doing this, I realized I was still being more of an observer than a true participant. Near the end of the service, my attention was pulled towards the altar and the Monstrance the priest was holding high above his head. As I was watching this, I noticed something very strange beginning to happen. The red center of the Monstrance that holds the consecrated host began pulsating as if it was a heart beating. I could not take my eyes off of it. I didn't know what to make of this and I looked around wondering if anyone else was seeing what I was seeing. Then I heard "The Voice" again. It was the same Voice I heard on Live Oak Plantation Road. This time it was a clear, gentle command that said "Take off your glasses so others may see Me as you saw Me!" I didn't know what to do with this, but I knew what I had heard, and I immediately pulled my sunglasses off my face. Instantly, I was hit with the harsh glare of the sun. It was so bright I could hardly open my eyes. I began to quickly look around me to see if anyone was looking at me. I didn't know what this meant and I didn't know what God wanted me to do beyond removing my glasses. I wondered if there was someone in the crowd I was supposed to see or who was supposed to see me. I was perplexed thinking I was supposed to do something but I had no idea what. All I was told was "Take off your glasses so others may see Me as you saw Me."

The Adoration Service ended and I must have had a bewildered look on my face because Judy looked at me and asked me what was going on, to which I hesitantly replied, "Something else just happened again." I was not sure I should tell her but I just could not keep this in. "I just heard this voice say loud and clear to 'Take off your glasses so others may see Me as you saw Me.' I don't know what I'm supposed to do. I think I need to talk to a priest."

Judy quickly turned to Terri and told her what had just happened and that I wanted to talk to a priest. Throughout all of this Terri amazed me with not only how she accepted this but also how she seemed to somehow expect it. She immediately left, only to re-emerge within just a few minutes. She grabbed my hand and said, "Come with me. I found you a priest." I followed Terri for a few yards and standing there in the hot sun was a priest that looked like Burl Ives. Terri boldly introduced me, "Father, this is my friend Don. He needs to talk to you. He has had some incredible experiences since we have been here and he would like to talk to a priest." He just nodded his head and held out his hand to me and said, "Let's see if we can find a place to sit somewhere out of this sun." He motioned for me to follow him and we walked around to the east side of the church where there were two empty confessional chairs beside the outside wall. The sun was beginning to set in the west and St. James cast a welcomed shadow for us. As we sat down, he introduced himself to me and told me he was from Detroit. I informed him that I was Protestant and explained our story to him beginning with Judy's prayer up to what had just happened during the Adoration Service. This priest would be the first of several men of the cloth that I would seek to help shed some spiritual knowledge on the things I had witnessed. I desperately needed help discerning what I was supposed to do concerning these experiences. I was not completely sure how this priest was receiving everything I was telling him. He was very attentive, almost expressionless, as I told him everything. I assumed that this is what priests do but I was beginning to feel a little self-conscious. Then, from a stoic stare, the priest melted. Before I could finish, a single trail of tears began to work their path down his cheek and onto his shirt. He told me he had been a priest for all of his adult life and had prayed for such an experience to happen to him. Nothing had ever happened to him in that way and I could sense his deep longing but also his grace. His words humbled and perplexed me. I still did not understand, why me? Why not someone like this good priest who was more deserving?

We eventually reached a point of departure. This had not been a confession nor did I gain any spiritual insight into my experiences. It had been more like two brothers sharing, each receiving from God. For me, this was an entirely new and unexpected experience. It did not matter that he was a Catholic priest and I was a backslidden Baptist. We were both brothers in Christ here and we believed in the same

God and sought the same Savior. The sharing touched and ministered to both of us.

I began to think I should leave to see if I could find Judy and Terri. He blessed me as I was leaving and I spontaneously blessed him back. I am sure this was probably not what a Catholic parishioner's response would have been to a priest. At that moment, whether it was or not didn't seem to matter. It came from the heart and I was glad to be free to do what seemed natural rather than be concerned with protocol.

Our parting moment still abides with me all these years later. I had gone to him looking for answers, but I left believing God had used me to give this priest a gift as well. It was a totally new experience for me to be used by Christ. I walked away with no answers as to what the Voice meant. I didn't know if these were literal words or more of a statement of how I was to live my life. The words haunted me the rest of my time in Medjugorje and it would not be until I got home that these words began to reveal their literal meaning.

I looked around for Judy and Terri and realized they had probably gone to the Rosary prayer. Wanting to be alone with my thoughts, I decided to walk on back to our place and wait on them to return for our evening meal. When I got back to the house I was met by two surprises. The first thing

I noticed was a stack of luggage sitting in the dining room. "Hysterical", I thought to myself, "just in time to pack and go home." As I was checking to make sure our bags were among those in the stack, a young man by the name of Mike said, "Hello." I had met Mike earlier and he had been waiting at the house for me to return so he could talk to me. Mike was also from Tallahassee but he had experienced a lot of difficulties traveling to Medjugorje and his entire trip had to be rerouted. This had caused him to arrived a couple of days later than the rest of us. He already knew several people in our group and some of them had told him about what had happened to me at Fr. Jozo's church. We struck up an interesting conversation and he began pouring things out to me about his life and the struggles he too had been having with his faith. We talked for over an hour, until our host family began making preparations for the evening meal. We decided to move our conversation out onto the small courtyard just off the dining room to wait for the others, who would be making their way back soon.

JUDY

After leaving Don with the priest Terri found me waiting on the West side of the church, which seemed to be a popular gathering place for many people to meet after the service. There were numerous groups in this area standing around and talking. When Terri caught up to me we discussed whether we should wait for Don or head over to the area where they would be praying the afternoon Rosary. As we were trying to decide what to do, I heard a woman from behind me say, "Oh My" and I turned around just in time to see her put her hand to her mouth and tell her friend to look at the sun. Her friend looked toward the sun and her mouth fell open. Terri and I quickly turned to see if we could see what they were looking at and Terri exclaimed, "Look, can you see that? It's the Miracle of the Sun." I looked and saw nothing but a glare and the sun was too bright to keep looking. I kept trying to look at the sun several times but I couldn't without the glare hurting my eyes. In a few minutes Terri said, "Hold my hand and look again" so I did. By this simple act it was as if the grace she had been given was passed to me and in an instant I, too, could see this miracle that so many people had witnessed while in Medjugorje. It looked as if the host, the round white wafer you receive during communion, had covered the sun to keep the glaring rays from hurting my eyes. You could see it pulsing and moving slightly over the center of the sun and the rays were diffused and coming out from the outer edges of the sun. It was incredible and we just stood there in silence along with the other two women behind us for several minutes. I looked around expecting to find everyone in the courtyard looking at the sun only to find that others in the area were oblivious to what we were witnessing.

Two women witnessing the Miracle of the Sun

I was so excited and couldn't wait to tell Don and the others that we too had seen the miracle many others had witnessed here since the beginning of the apparitions. We stood there for a while just watching in awe. At some point I began to notice many people were leaving the courtyard and walking toward the front of St. James. I knew most of them were headed to pray the afternoon Rosary. In that moment, we realized it might be some time before Don would join us, so we decided we would go ahead and join the others and pray the Rosary. As we walked away, we continued to look back several times to see if we could still see this miracle.

Each time we looked back, it was still there for us. Once we reached the east side of St. James we could no longer see the sun, so we found a place to sit and waited for the Rosary to begin.

As incredible as it was to witness the Miracle of the Sun, I still couldn't shake my concern for Don. Just by observing him, I knew he was trying to understand everything that had happened to him. He was much quieter and more reflective. In a different way, I was trying to process it all too. His experiences had not happened to me but I was there. I had witnessed it happen and I had heard everything first hand. I saw the immediate effect it had on him and I too was walking into the reality of this spiritual world that was greater than I could have ever imagined possible. I couldn't stop thinking about the voice he had heard at the Adoration Service and I was wondering if the priest was helping him gain any understanding of what the message might have meant.

In the midst of all these thoughts, someone began leading us in the Rosary. As we were praying the Rosary, my mind began to drift between everything that had happened to us here and the realization that tomorrow we would be leaving Medjugorje. The people in our group had experienced so many wonderful gifts and miracles and almost everyone had been commenting on how they didn't want to leave. I felt somewhat different. It wasn't that I truly wanted to leave this beautiful place that was full of so much prayer and where God's graces were being poured out. It was that I clearly needed to go where I could just quietly rest with God and let everything sink in. I wanted to be alone, just me and God, outside under a beautiful sky or by a quiet stream and simply contemplate the magnitude of all we had witnessed.

At the completion of the Rosary, everyone in our group began to walk back toward the house in groups of two or three. As we turned the corner to go toward our place, I noticed ahead that Don and his new friend were standing outside talking on the patio. Page was just a few feet ahead of me when I heard Don call out to her and say "Page, look up at the cross on the mountain." As Page turned to look, I saw her put her hand over her mouth looking just as shocked as the two women in the courtyard, who just an hour earlier had witnessed the Miracle of the Sun. I rushed to join them to see what they were looking at and just as I looked toward the top of Cross Mountain the cross appeared to be turning on its base. I say "appeared" because there was no way in reality that it was possible. I had been up to this mountain and leaned on this sixteen ton cross. I had walked all around it. It was solid and planted heavily into the solid ground. But there it was turning as if waving goodbye to everyone on our last day. Don never said, "Look, the cross is turning." We had simply been told to look and simultaneously everyone saw the cross turn.

There was a young girl from New Jersey, who was a member of the U.S. Olympic team that had joined us, along with her mother. She began to excitedly jump up and down and repeatedly shout, "Look! Look!" Every time the cross turned, she would continue to scream. It was one more incredible gift and I will never forget everyone's joy at being able to share in this experience together. We realized this would be our last night in Medjugorje and that seemed to make sharing this experience even more meaningful to all of us.

After a while, we finally pulled ourselves away, as we were being called in for our last dinner together in Medjugorje. Everyone at dinner seemed to be full of so much love and joy and the conversation was filled with excitement. I was feeling all of this myself; however, it was also mixed with a growing sense of sadness at the thought of leaving. On this last evening, nearly everyone had now experienced some form of a supernatural event. This trip had given all of us incredible evidence of God's presence in our world. For a short period of time we had all been living in the present moment with no concerns about tomorrow. I thought about Terri and how all of this must have been a touching confirmation of her own faith in delivering Mary's message to us. I knew both Don and I would forever feel grateful to her and thanked God for her obedience and courage in stepping out in faith to bring me Mary's invitation.

> Oh, how great are God's riches, and
> wisdom, and knowledge! How impossible
> it is for us to understand his decisions and
> his ways!
>
> Romans 11:33
> New Living Translation

Chapter 17

Saying Good-Bye

Our host family waving good-bye

JUDY

*A*fter dinner, most of us walked back outside onto the
patio to relax awhile and talk. Don and I found our-

selves in a conversation with Lois, who I felt had in many ways become the matriarch of our group. She was the first one that had come to Medjugorje and she always seemed to be so calm and content in her demeanor. She also seemed to have a very mature and strong faith. As we were talking on the patio with Lois, Don mentioned to her how before coming to Medjugorje I had written down all my prayers and that every one of them had been answered. And indeed they had. The transformation of Don through his vision of Christ at Fr. Jozo's church in Tihaljina was more than I had even imagined possible or would have dared to have asked for. He was a different person. He was at peace and he was speaking in ways I had never heard him speak before. But it was more than just that. His face was softer; he had a new innocence about him. He was like someone who had just been born or awakened into this new spiritual world. He had seen and felt the presence of God and it was no longer an idea but a reality that he had never experienced before. I was able to watch him walk into it like a baby taking their first steps. He was walking around sure of what had happened to him but unsure of what he was to do next or what he was to do with the gifts he had been given.

As we talked about our week with Lois, I remember commenting to her that when I came to Medjugorje I had felt content and that I needed nothing because the moment when

Terri sat down in my office, three months earlier, my prayers had been answered. Through that conversation with Terri and her invitation from Mary, God had given me what I needed. I knew He was there and that He was still with me. I knew He had heard my prayer. Somewhere in my heart I felt all along that, even though I had been the one invited to come by the Blessed Virgin Mary, this trip was going to be special for Don. I don't know how I perceived this but there was something in my spirit that gave me peace about this. I had a peace within me the whole time he had been protesting about going before the trip and I never really worried about whether he would go or not. For once, I really knew that God was in control of this and not me.

Having just said all of this to Lois, the realization hit me like a ton of bricks. This really was our last evening in Medjugorje and tomorrow we would be leaving this place of special graces and I didn't know if I would ever be back. Unexpectedly, I began to choke on my own words....did I really mean what I had just said? Did I really need nothing more? Maybe I didn't need more but suddenly, I found myself wanting something more. I realized I wanted my own personal hug from my Heavenly Father before we left this place where God was pouring His love out on so many. I began to feel anxious at the thought of leaving without this and found myself making up an excuse to dismiss myself from the conversation and strike out on my own toward St. James. The sun was setting as I walked into an open field to the right of the church. Alone, in the middle of this field, I fell down on my knees with my face in my hands, crying and I prayed....."Father, you have given me so much, more than I ever deserve, more than I could ever dream to ask for. It should be enough and it is. I said that I needed nothing more than what You have already given me but now we are getting ready to leave and I find myself wanting more. I need my own special touch from my Heavenly Father before I leave." Tears were flowing as I came to terms with the fact that this was my last night in Medjugorje. I came with prayer for many other people but I had not been asking anything specific for me. Now realizing we were about to leave I knew I wanted something more. I wanted anything that the Lord would give me. After I had been there a while, pouring my heart out, I realized it was beginning to get very dark. Resigning myself to be content with what I had already received, I headed back to our house to begin packing for home.

After Don and I had finished packing and getting every-thing ready to leave, he told me his new friend, Mike, had wanted to climb Cross Mountain before he had to leave. Don had told Mike that he would go up with him. He asked me if I wanted to go with them but I declined because it was night and getting late. I was completely exhausted from the emotions of this last day. Remembering that Don's hiking boots had finally arrived with our luggage, I suggested that he should wear them, especially in the dark. Don smiled at me and said, "We've decided to go up barefoot." I had to laugh. After Don and Mike left, Terri found me and asked me if I wanted to walk to the church one last time to which I replied "Yes". We took our time slowly walking toward St. James and, once there, we began looking around and saying hello to others who were also out enjoying the summer evening. We were walking around the west side courtyard when I saw Terri walk toward the window where the Virgin Mary had appeared to her on her first trip in May. I knew exactly what she was thinking and what she was feeling without her saying a word. She stood up on the bench and gazed into the window for several minutes as one would look out at the sea wishing to see a loved one's ship coming into sight. But within a few minutes, she stepped down resigned, as if she knew this would probably not happen again. She looked like I was feeling- sad to be leaving and hoping that maybe, just maybe, she would be able to see her one more time. We decided to walk around to an area behind the church where there was an entrance to a cemetery. As we were standing at the top of the steps, leading down into the cemetery, two young men who looked to be in their early twenties were coming up the steps. We said our greetings and they stopped to exchange some casual conversation with us. We learned they were two American seminary students studying to become priests. They told us they had walked to the back of the church to pray a Rosary and asked if we would like to join them. The four of us sat down on the steps staring out into the darkness as we began to pray the Rosary together. We knew that right in front of us in the distance was Cross Mountain but it was pitch black so we couldn't see anything this night, not even the outline of the mountain. After we had been praying for a little while, we all suddenly stopped the prayer as we gasped at what we simultaneously saw in the sky above the top of the cross. There were three short bursts of pure light that lit up the area on and around the cross on Cross Mountain. The light came from as high as you could see into the sky and looked like a huge spotlight from heaven had been turned on three separate times in quick succession. The light was in the shape of a massive funnel that was wide at the top and became narrow at the bottom, as it shown directly on the cross. Immediately after this, the cross itself lit up with the purest white light, unlike any light I had ever seen before. We could not contain our excitement as we kept saying to each other, "Did you see that? Did you see that?" It was as if we needed reassurance of the miracle we had just witnessed together. Someone said the visionaries had once been asked the question of what happens when the Virgin Mary appears to them. They had *answered that before she comes there are always three quick burst of light. I had never heard this before. Someone else said the visionaries also said that the Virgin Mary often prayed at the base of the cross. Could it be that we all just witnessed this light and could it be that she was there now? Seeing this made everything in the Bible come alive - the parting of the Red Sea, God speaking to Moses through a burning bush, Jesus turning water into wine...suddenly these were not nice stories from Sunday School but I was seeing the same awesome power of God right here before my own eyes.*

I can't remember if we finished praying the Rosary or if we were just too excited. I remember we talked for a short while still in awe of what we had just shared and then we hugged these two strangers who had witnessed this beautiful miracle with us good-bye. Terri and I could not wait to get back to tell the others and then I remembered, Don was actually on the mountain while all this was going on. I began to wonder what he might have seen. On the way home, it was obvious that our sadness had turned to joy. In looking back at this moment, I can somehow relate to how the two Mary's must have felt when they discovered Jesus' empty tomb. They had gone to the tomb in deep sadness but when they encountered the risen Lord they also had rushed back with joy to tell the others.

After returning to our place and telling the others what we witnessed I went to bed with the greatest joy that once again my Father had heard my prayer and He had given me a beautiful parting gift. I don't know what time it was when Don got back in because I was sound asleep. He woke me up as he was trying to get in the bed and I mumbled, "Did you see anything when you were on the mountain?" He replied, "I didn't see anything but when we got to the top there was a sudden strong breeze that came through- much like what the visionaries describe and what we felt the first day during the apparition. I heard someone whisper that the Virgin is here praying and others made their way toward the base of the cross to say a Rosary." I smiled but I was too tired to tell Don what we had witnessed. That would have to wait until tomorrow, as I went back to my peaceful and fully content sleep.

It would not be until I was back home in Tallahassee that I would realize that this special good-bye gift was not all that God had in store for me. I remembered Don saying Jesus had told him that some of us would receive gifts while in Medjugorje and some of us would receive gifts when we returned home. I also remembered Don turning to Terri on Apparition Hill and telling her that he knew what my gift would be. He had whispered it into Terri's ear but he would not tell me. I remembered what had started this journey of ours to faith; it was all the miscarriages, the ectopic pregnancy, the disappointment and fear that I would never be able to carry a baby to term. It was the feeling of being abandoned by God which had caused all my doubts and then the prayers that God had heard and answered. I remember Don saying Jesus had told him that we may not necessarily get what we ask for but we would get what we need the most. Within two weeks of being home, it was confirmed that I was pregnant. Our joy at this news was uncontainable and I knew in my heart that this was the most precious and special gift I could ever receive. Don confirmed this when he finally told me that Jesus had told him my gift was going to be a son. Knowing this, I had no doubts that this time the baby I was carrying within me would also be held in my arms. My doctor who had been with me through all the miscarriages and the ectopic pregnancy wanted me to be extremely cautious- both emotionally and physically. While sitting in her office I asked her if she believed in miracles and I proceeded to tell her about our trip to Medjugorje along with the message that Jesus gave to Don about my gift. She looked at me squarely and said that she did not discount miracles at all. With that, I assured her everything was going to be OK. When she spoke to me about the optional Amniotic Fluid Test to check for possible birth defects I declined the test because it posed certain risk factors. Even though the risk was very low I assured her the test results would make no difference to me and that I would never consider aborting this child even if the results of the test were positive for birth defects. She could see that I was firm in my decision and even though I was thirty-five she did not push the issue. I could not wait to get to the office and tell Terri my news. As soon as I found Terri I pulled her in my office and burst out with the news, "I'm pregnant". We shared a joyful hug in my office as she told me that Don had said this would be my gift.

With a few months Don went with me to the doctor for my first sonogram and it was confirmed, just as Don had been told, that I was in fact going to have a son. Throughout the pregnancy I had never felt better nor had I been happier. On April 23, 1991 our son, Devon Powell Bailey was born, three and a half weeks early. I will never forget the ride to the hospital as I looked over at Don and saw his excitement as he silently made a motion with his fist in the air like, "All right, the moment I've been waiting for". The joy and the gratitude I felt at that moment was over whelming and I could hardly hold it in. The excitement over the prospect of finally holding my son far outweighed any fear of what the next few hours might be like. I called my longtime and dear friend Margaret, who was a mid-wife and prenatal nurse and she rushed to be with me throughout the labor and delivery. She was an absolute Godsend as she kept all the nurses on the floor jumping at every need I had. When Devon was finally placed in my arms and I was able to see him for the first time it was as if I was looking at someone whom I had known forever. The bonding felt instant and I was overcome with an emotion of a type of love I had never felt before.

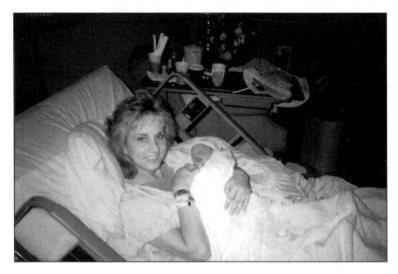

Judy with our Medjugorje gift

It was clear. God knew my heart's deepest desire and He knew this is what I needed most of all to feel complete. I have often thought of the vision that Don saw of my mother and the Virgin Mary and how he said mama had turned and looked at him with a smile. In my heart I believe that she was smiling because she knew what was to come. In my heart I believe that Mary was comforting her and telling her that I would have a child- something that my mother would have wanted for me more than anything. The connection between my Heavenly Mother, my earthly mother and me becoming a mother did not go unnoticed by me. Only mothers could really understand how much I desired this and I believe they prayed for me like all good mothers would. I will be eternally grateful and give thanks to the Father for answering their prayer on my behalf.

Looking back at these miraculous events and the tremendous love and grace we received from our Heavenly Father I still cannot tell you why God moves the way He does. All I know is that I was asked to go and I said yes to that call. I know there are special graces and amazing signs and wonders there. I know the prayers in Medjugorje are so thick that you can physically feel them in the atmosphere as soon as you arrive. I don't know why we received these gifts. Perhaps it was to be a messenger to you, the reader, that God exists, that He hears our prayers, and that we are all important to Him. This is one of the earliest messages from the Virgin Mary to the Children when she was asked why she was appearing in Medjugorje. She told them- "I have come to tell the world that God exists."

God comes to each of us in different ways but He is always waiting for us to respond and to remember Him. To remember who He is and to remember what He has done for us. I don't know what your need is right now but I needed faith. I had almost lost mine. We can ask for many things but without faith we have no lasting anchor. I prayed..."God, if you want me, you're going to have to come down here and show me...I'm trying and I'm having a hard time believing anymore." Some people are shocked at this prayer but I am reminded of Scripture in the Bible where a man brought his son to Jesus to be healed and Jesus asked this father "How long has this been happening to him?" And he said, "From childhood. But, if you can do anything, have compassion on us and help us." And Jesus said to him, "If you can? All things are possible for one who believes." Immediately the father of the child cried out and said, "I believe; yet help my unbelief!" (Mark 9:21-23) In a very real way that is what I was asking too. From my childhood my faith had been challenged from time to time by things I could not understand. Still I had just enough faith to cry out and say, "I need to know, help my unbelief"

Too many people today are trying to erase the true existence of God. Relying upon their intellect only, they believe and want you to believe that faith is for the weak or superstitious. We are here to tell you our story and to say that He does exist and He wants us all to seek Him in our doubts, our wounds and our pains.

I cried out of the depths of confusion, frustration and the pain of not knowing for sure. Through the Virgin Mary, God called us to Medjugorje and there she pointed the way to Jesus, her Son. It was a beautiful and heavenly orchestrated plan.

I don't know where you are today. Perhaps you have doubts just like I did. Maybe you also have an image of God that's not true, hidden behind years of religiosity. Perhaps you can't yet believe how much He is ready to embrace you and to help you in your own struggles and that He longs for you to know Him intimately. Perhaps there is a message for you, too, coming out of this tiny village in the former Yugoslavia.

O taste and see that the LORD is good;
how blessed is the man who takes refuge
in Him!

Psalm 34:8
New American Standard Bible

Chapter 18

The Journey That Never Ends

JUDY AND DON

T he end of our trip to Medjugorje marked the beginning of a new era in our lives. It is the point in time
from which we now measure our life. We left Medjugorje
with the renewed reality of our relationship with God our
Father, Jesus our Savior, and our guide, the Holy Spirit. It
was also the beginning of a new love and appreciation for
Mary, our heavenly mother. We wish we could report that
the last twenty-one years have been perfect and that we have
been perfect saintly people because of the beautiful gifts we
received, but that would not be true. Instead, our lives have
been a series of ups and downs- kind of like Don's vision
of the water flowing back and forth between himself and
Jesus. Jesus told Don the water flowing back and forth had
represented those times when he had drawn near Him and

those times when he had gone away. We have gone through times where we felt strongly that we were doing God's will. There were also times when we felt we had lost our direction and couldn't find our compass or understand what God was doing, if anything, with us. Looking back now, we know this is often the Christian walk of faith but we didn't understand that then. For us, there was a maturing in faith that needed to take place. We believe this is what Jesus was referring to when He told Don he did not yet have the capacity to understand everything. Many people assumed, because of these experiences, we were further along in our spiritual growth than we actually were. It would take a series of falling down and getting up to teach us we had much to learn.

As soon as we returned home we wanted to find a church. We both had been brought up in the Baptist Church, but our experience in Medjugorje had left us with a strong desire for the Eucharist and we felt drawn toward a church in which the Eucharist was the center of the service. We loved all our Baptist brothers and sisters and, in fact, Judy's family has ministers in this church. We feel our Baptist roots gave us a tremendous scriptural education and we in no way want our experience to project a negative light on our experience while attending this church. It is just that we both experienced a more meaningful and strong pull towards the Eucharist, and we left Medjugorje hungry for that. After visiting several churches, we felt very drawn to a particular Episcopal Church and more so to this church's welcoming priest. When we told him our story, he was visibly moved and told us that, while we had come to him in search of a church home, we had also brought him a gift. We were never sure exactly what he meant by that, but so often we would go looking for guidance or understanding and God would use us to minister to the person we were seeking answers from.

In many ways, when we first came back, it was very hard to focus on work. Terri and Judy found themselves going to lunch together often after returning home. Lunches that had usually been filled with conversations related to work were now spent talking about God and things associated with their faith. We all found ourselves looking around for miracles and, although they were there in small and sometimes unrecognized ways, they were not the magnitude of those we had witnessed while in Medjugorje. Fortunately, during these earlier years, it seemed God was taking care of everything while we continued to share this story as He placed people in front of us. It did seem we were under a special grace. As the word of our experience traveled, we found ourselves being invited to speak at a diverse group of churches including Catholic, Protestant and non-denominational churches. The word about Don's experience and the miracles we had witnessed on our trip also traveled quickly through our workplace. The interest in what had happened was at a high level and many were asking questions. To avoid disruption in the workplace by sharing our story over and over to one individual after the other, we decided to set up a meeting one evening in one of our homes. Everyone at Judy's office was invited to come as well as members of another office group who were interested in hearing our story. Many people who came said that hearing our story changed their lives. The Holy Spirit seemed to place people in need of our witness in front of us from every walk of our lives. Don would find himself talking to a group of men on one of his construction sites or, as people heard about our story, we would be invited to homes or out to dinner to share what had happened. Wherever we spoke, whether it was one on one with an individual or in a larger group, the presence of the Holy Spirit was always there and we knew lives were being touched. There were several times when Don spoke that people reported experiencing supernatural things happening to them. At one of our first meetings, a non-Christian reported seeing a glow around Don as he talked to a group in a home. After an impromptu testimony at Good Sheppard Catholic Church, several people in the audience reported seeing a golden aura around Don as he spoke. One man left a meeting speechless and we later learned he reported seeing Christ and had observed the wounds in his hands as Don's talked to the group. After a church gathering a woman fell forward into Don's arms, crying deep tears after hearing him speak. We were told the following day by friends of hers that she told them that, when she was about to leave, she had wanted to give Don a hug for sharing his story. When she went to hug him, she said she saw Christ embracing her in her spirit and was overcome by tears. Don was completely unaware when these things were happening. As we would hear about them, it began to give meaning to the message he had been given at the Adoration Service when he had been told to take off his glasses so others could see Jesus as he had seen Him. It was as if the presence of Jesus was still on Don and the Holy Spirit ministered to them and met their individual needs. This particular grace was reported most often in the first year after we returned from Medjugorje.

We aren't sure how long this went on because many times people would leave without saying anything. We would mistakenly think our message had not been received well, only to find out later that in fact those same people were deeply moved beyond words in their spirit. We began to realize it was not for us to try and gauge the reaction of a group or individuals. God had His own plan and appointed time for each person and what they received was from Him and not us. Wherever we spoke, we left feeling God's presence and always the joy of being used to tell the story God had given us. These opportunities always felt like divine appointments and left us with tremendous peace.

Once, when Don was speaking to the Men's Breakfast Group at our church, something unusual occurred with our son Devon who was three years old at the time. Devon was not feeling well that morning, so Don decided to take him to the breakfast meeting with him instead of pre-school. A friend of ours, Gary Gammon, who also was Devon's Godfather, sat near him and had given him some crayons and paper to keep him occupied while Don talked. A few weeks later, Gary brought us a picture he had collected from Devon's papers. Gary had found the drawing of our three year old remarkable, especially considering what Don had been talking about during the meeting. Gary wanted us to look at the picture to see if we saw what he was seeing in the childlike drawing. We were truly amazed to see a somewhat abstract, yet clear, image of the Virgin Mary. In fact, the drawing had three separate images of the Virgin Mary hidden within the one picture. Devon had placed childlike sun rays all around the image as if to give it light.

The Holy Spirit continued working in and through us for at least eight or nine more years, ministering to others in phenomenal ways. Still to this day, we find ourselves called to tell the story in some very unexpected situations and Don continues to receive messages from the Holy Spirit for others.

Looking back, we realize now that God's grace was on our sharing and this carried us in a special way during those early years. We also realize there was a power beyond our testimony that held the attention of those we spoke to and it ministered to them in ways we would have never known how to do. However, just like with any mountaintop experience, you must come down and live in the valley.

While writing this book, we wanted to be as honest and transparent as possible to let you know that we are not special people. We are like most people. We struggle with life, each other, work and relationships. We still struggle from time to time with issues of our faith as we learn to walk deeper into it. We are continuously challenged to trust more and more. We sometimes forget and still look to ourselves too often instead of God. There have been times when we have let the cares of the world begin to choke out the things of God. We have also suffered the loss of meaningful relationships. At times, we were so caught up in these things that we even forgot to live the beautiful messages we had heard in Medjugorje. During those times, the demands on us were overwhelming and we found ourselves spending less and less time with God. We found ourselves striving with each more and getting caught up in the trappings of the world. Never, however, during any of these times, have we been able to suppress the memories of what God did for us and how he had answered Judy's prayers. Never have we forgotten the miraculous way in which He reached down in such a personal way to show Don his love and acceptance. Never have we forgotten the gift of our son and the blessing he has been. These memories, along with the faithfulness of our God, have always brought us back when we strayed or found ourselves drifting off course. God has always remained faithful, even when we were weak. Jesus was never the one that moved away- it was always us. We now understand that God allows us to go through periods of drought to teach us and help us grow, as well as to test us. We discovered that too much reliance on or comfort in the things of the world is not only deceiving but also fleeting. This happened to us and we fell into our own time of testing and drought.

Our test (or drought) began when things that had helped support us began to fall apart in different ways. The priest we had felt so close to was suddenly gone from our church, and many of the services and people we had been connected to began to change. The Episcopal Church itself experienced its own set of problems, as we believe many leaders in the church began to deny foundational scriptural truths. The church was in turmoil and we found ourselves disenfranchised with everything going on within the structure of this church. At the same time, the work that Judy had enjoyed for so many years found itself in a transition as well when large corporations moved in. Judy's days would often start at 7:30 a.m. and go late into the evenings. The joy of developing clients and employee relationships became more difficult. She was working longer and longer hours managing reports and inventory rather than continuing to develop people on her staff. She was deeply distressed that her career was dominating her life and leaving little time for family. In 2006, Judy accepted another job within her company and we moved to Sarasota, Florida. Don joined a real estate firm there just at the moment the housing bubble burst and it seemed that Sarasota was ground zero. We had purchased a beautiful home on a lake in Tallahassee just five months before Judy was transferred. We were now living like Gypsies from apartment to apartment in Sarasota, as the radio station would barter advertising for us a place to stay. The stress during this time was tremendous and the strain was hard on our marriage. Sometimes, it seemed that our relationship was not going to bear up under all the pressure as we found ourselves growing more frustrated with each other and our circumstances. Our son, Devon, was participating in rowing events and we would often be out of town traveling on weekends or Don would be on the road back to Tallahassee to check on our property there. Without realizing it, we had allowed our circumstances and the long hours of work to slowly but surely crowd out the things of God.

Within seventeen months of the move, Judy's position was eliminated. At the end of 2007, we decided to move back into our home in Tallahassee to allow Devon, who was then fifteen, to finish high school there. After moving back to Tallahassee, we found a new home in the Anglican Church. With fewer demands and distractions for Judy she slowed down long enough to feel God's tug on her heart. She began thinking about the time of joy we had shared when we both felt we were being used by God. While looking through an old photo album of our trip to Medjugorje, she pulled out a photograph of the two of us and placed it on her bathroom mirror. The photo was taken at a small cafe located on the Adriatic Sea about an hour and a half after leaving Medjugorje. In a few days, Don noticed the picture and asked her why she had put it there. She told him that it reminded her of a time when they were at their best and she was the happiest.

The photo Judy placed on her mirror to remember the blessings of their time in Medjugorje. Taken at a cafe by the Adriatic on their way home.

She also made a call to reconnect with Bob Schuchts to discuss a dilemma she was facing and he reminded her of the things she had learned in Medjugorje. Bob suggested she begin praying the Rosary again. He also extended an invitation for us to attend a series of classes he was teaching. Halfway through his course, there was a teaching on God's Redemption and we were invited to tell our story during this class. Although we had continued to tell our story to individuals from time to time, as we felt lead by God's promptings, this would be the first time in several years that we would again share our story in a public setting. Little did we know at the time that this would be the start of another season for us going deeper with God. It was also during this time that we began to feel called to write this book.

We have discovered that our walk with God is not always a direct path. It has been a path of learning, with boulders and thorn bushes all along the way. Each of these obstacles represented an opportunity to learn and grow and then move forward. We began to learn that just like on Cross Mountain we occasionally needed to pause and take a look around to notice where we are and where God might be leading us.

In 2009, Don attended a men's group retreat called Return to Glory. The four day retreat was based on the book called *"Wild at Heart"* written by John Eldredge. Throughout this weekend, he ventured for the first time into some of the deepest wounds in his heart. This experience brought healing and a new sense of God fulfilling His purpose in Don's life. Also during this time period, Judy was able to reconnect to things that were hidden in her heart as well. She has become a Guardian Ad Litum volunteer, representing children from abused or neglected homes within the court system and she is also enjoying serving on a Healing and Prayer Ministry Team.

Our son, Devon, is now twenty years old and we can see God working in his life. He is a sophomore in college and has a passion for making films. He also has a deep faith and has grown into his own relationship with God. Currently, he is a Young Life Leader sharing the love of Christ with middle school students.

Our son Devon 2011

Over the years, we have been encouraged to write our story and we always believed this was something we needed to do. We also believe that God has given us this time together to write. We don't know why the time is now but we both believe it's God's timing and not ours. God has used the writing of this book to continue His work, both through us and in each of us. We are still amazed at how efficient God is. Just like our trip to Medjugorje, the process of writing this book has been both a personal journey for each of us, while at the same time another journey together. God has continued to minister and reveal more to us during this process. He has continued to teach us more about ourselves and each other. Never have we spent so much time with each other, and we have continued to learn how God uses us, comes to us and loves us, even when we do not feel worthy.

In Medjugorje, we realized that no one happens to go there by chance. We believe the same is also true for those reading this book. It is no more of an accident that you picked up this book (or that someone gave it to you) than it was that we ended up in the village of Medjugorje. There are no accidents when God is involved, only divine appointments. This is how it has been since the first time we shared our story. It is our deep prayer that, through this book, Christ has spoken to your heart and that your heart was open to hear whatever it most needed to hear.

In this you rejoice, although now for
a little while you may have to suffer
through various trials, so that the genuineness of your faith, more precious than
gold that is perishable even though tested
by fire, may prove to be for praise, glory,
and honor at the revelation
of Jesus Christ.

I Peter 1:6-7
The New American Bible

Chapter 19

Heart Reflections

Don and Judy

Over the past twenty-one years, we have both been asked many questions about our experiences. We have had many years to look back and reflect on the supernatural and mystical events we experienced in Medjugorje and that are reported to be continuing still today. When we first began the writing of this book, we did not feel it was our mission to try and prove to you that the Virgin Mary is appearing to six children, now adults. Many books have already been written on this subject, giving full accounts in great details of the six visionaries, the priests there, and the messages they continue to receive for themselves and for the world. There is, however, strong and compelling evidence of the overflowing of God's grace on those who go to Medjugorje.

The visionaries have undergone incredible scrutiny by the Catholic Church as well as medical, scientific and psychological experts. People have tried to prove, and some have tried to disprove, the things going on in Medjugorje. Some have suggested that the occurrences are not of God and rather His enemy, Satan. The best response we have ever heard to that is that if this is of Satan then he has converted, because everything there points to Jesus, to reading the Bible, to attending church, to fasting and a return to love. As we consider all this, we cannot help but remember how Jesus was treated by the religious and political leaders of his time. Most of the studies and tests conclude there is something of a physiological nature going on when the visionaries are in front of the apparition of the Virgin Mary. None of these experts can prove scientifically the apparitions are real, but then again they have not been able to prove they aren't. In the end, it is still a matter of faith for each of us.

All we can do is look at the amazing fruits and the multitude of lives that have been changed. All we can do is look at what it has done and what it has meant in our own lives. All we can do is tell you our story, and it is impossible to tell our story without shining a light on the Virgin Mary's role in it. We believe our story demonstrates how much our Father loves us (all of us) and the lengths He is willing to go to demonstrate that love. We believe He is moved to action when we cry out to Him with a sincere heart that wants to truly know Him. We believe that, in Judy's prayer, God knew she was trying to understand and trying to hear but she had allowed many things to get in the way of a true relationship with Him. Because she couldn't reach Him in a tangible way, she was beginning to doubt it all. She wanted Him to intervene and help her know the truth – she almost demanded it.

Don, on the other hand, didn't really expect much from God and had accepted a very sterile form of Christianity that was only on the surface and not very deep. For him, the extent of his Christian experience had hinged on the Bible verse, John 3:16, for salvation through believing that Jesus was the Son of God. Most of the teachings that Don had been exposed to focused primarily on salvation rather than an ongoing and ever-growing relationship with God or Christian charismatic gifts. Don had accepted a belief that everything we need is contained in the Bible and any connection God made with man, as in the burning bush or the cloud leading the Israelites in the desert or angelic messengers, was for that time and that time only. He even wondered if those things literally happened or instead were metaphors for interpretation. As far as Don was concerned, God was definitely not doing "those" things in our world today. Don's theology, like many socially accepted forms of

Christianity today, had placed limits on what God would do. In essence, he had placed God in a small box.

How often do we all find ourselves doing the same thing, settling in on a form of Christianity that makes us feel good but never takes us into a deeper knowledge or relationship with God? How often do we settle in on a convenient view of God, picking and choosing what parts we like or don't like and in essence creating a god of our own making? How often do we think of God as only found in the Bible or in a church, and when we need our weekly or monthly or yearly fix, we know where to go visit Him; kind of like calling a friend we've avoided for a while.

We have learned, first hand, that you cannot put our living God in a box. He cannot simply be contained in the Bible or a church building. He certainly will not be contained in the idols that we create of him to suit our own image of what we want God to be. God is who He is. He created us and we do not get to create Him to fit into our own self-made and acceptable containers. He works in all places and in all our churches where people are open to Him and where it is evident through the working of the Holy Spirit. He can be found on a construction site or in an unfamiliar village, in former Yugoslavia, in an unfamiliar church, among unfamiliar traditions. If God can accept all of us wherever we are, should we not do the same with each other? Through these experiences and so many others, God is saying I am here and I want you to know I love you. That is why I created you. He wants us to seek for more of Him and to give more of ourselves back to Him. If the relationship is to be meaningful and fruitful we have to participate.

Neither of us, when we went to Medjugorje, had any prior knowledge of other Marian apparitions anywhere else in the world. We had never heard of Fatima, Lourdes or Guadeloupe. Don only slightly remembered a brief TV clip of the events taking place in Medjugorje. We were, however, both well acquainted with the anti-Catholic sentiments that can be found among some Protestants. In fact, Judy has a Christmas vase with the image of the Virgin Mary and Child trimmed in gold filigree which belonged to her mother. Her sister, who was several years older, told her that their father never liked the vase because it was "too Catholic" looking. When Judy's mother died, in a Catholic hospital in Atlanta, Judy asked the hospital to call in an Episcopal priest, thinking her mother would have preferred that.

Conversely, we have also run across Catholics who want to argue why they are right and others are all wrong. It is not the purpose of this book to debate either side of this issue because at the foot of the Cross in Medjugorje we were all together brothers and sisters in Christ. We felt clearly that

God is more concerned with our hearts than he is with our doctrines. Everyone who comes to believe at the foot of the cross with an opened heart, regardless of church or doctrine, becomes one in Him who died for us all.

During our trip, we learned we had many misunderstandings about some of the Catholic practices and traditions. In reference to Mary, many outside of the Catholic Church believe Catholic's worship Mary. We found that, while our Catholic friends did honor her role in the church, they do not worship her and we were able to see and understand the difference. We saw no one placed Mary ahead of Jesus, but instead we came to see her as an advocate and one of the best prayer partners you could ever have.

For us, there can be no denying that She is more than just a character in the Bible that Protestants typically talk about during Christmas. She is so much more. She is the one chosen by God to give birth to His Son. She is the one who said, "Yes" to the Holy Spirit. She is the Ark of the New Covenant. She was trusted by God to nurture and teach Jesus as a young child. She was there, prompting Jesus to perform his first public miracle. She was also there at the foot of His Cross when those who were closest to Him had fled. She was there with the apostles at Pentecost, when the Holy Spirit was breathed on them. Jesus asked John to behold her as His mother as one of His last requests before He died on the cross. We believe, in essence, He was offering her as Mother to all of us. We cannot deny that Judy was invited by the Virgin Mary through an employee who had no idea of the spiritual struggle that Judy was going through at the time. What more can we say? This is evidence to us that, just like Jesus, His mother is concerned for the world and for all of us in it. In fact, this is exactly what the visionary Ivan had said when he was asked if she had made comments about non-Catholics that do not follow the teaching of the Roman Catholic Church. He told us that Mary had said that she was here as the "Mother of All the World and that her message was for all faiths and people." We believe that, in our case and in the case of Medjugorje, the messages given there have pointed the way not to her but back to Jesus.

To our Protestant brothers and sisters we would say, consider what is going on in Medjugorje with an open heart. As evidence of our story and the many others, the graces there are not just for Catholics, and Catholics are not the only ones being called there. Many people from various religious backgrounds have come to faith in Jesus while in Medjugorje. In fact, the statue of Mary on Apparition Hill was erected by a Buddhist family whose child was healed there.

One question we are often asked is, "Why do you think God gave you these gifts and choose to reveal himself to you in such a miraculous way?" We have asked ourselves the same question many times and there have been many, many times that we felt so unworthy of these incredible gifts. The only way we know how to answer this is to tell you what the visionaries said when they asked the Virgin Mary why She had chosen them. Her reply was, "My little ones, God does not always choose the best people." We can only say with tremendous humility that this holds true for us.

Another question we have been asked is, why were we called to Medjugorje? We know that Jesus will meet you wherever you seek him, and you certainly do not have to go to Medjugorje or anywhere else to experience His love. Medjugorje is a place where people from all over the world come together united in faith and deep prayer. It is also a place of Christian love and joy. People are called to Medjugorje from every nation for many reasons. Some go seeking physical healings or healing from wounds of their hearts. Others go with family concerns. Most, however, go because they sense a need for peace in their soul or they have a desire to experience a deeper awareness of God. Many simply feel a call in their heart. Not everyone that goes to Medjugorje sees a miracle or experiences anything supernatural, but it is impossible not to experience the peace and serenity observed in those who are there. Most leave knowing they have experienced the presence of God.

Medjugorje is a place where special graces are flowing, and when we were there it was a place of solitude without the distractions and attachments of our busy world. Perhaps God knew our hearts needed such a place to become still and soak in the heavy prayer in order to open up. In all the years since, we have found we often feel His presence the strongest when we get quiet for periods of time and become steeped in deep prayer. This holds especially true in the community of other believers who are also seeking His presence.

All we really know is what we have shared with you in the pages of this book. We were called to Medjugorje by Mary, the Mother of Christ and everything there exalted the Lord Jesus Christ. We believe we are just messengers of His truth. We believe He is the Good Shepherd that leaves His flock and goes after the one lost sheep. There are no doubts, looking around at what is going on in the world today that many have lost their way and desperately need to find peace, meaning or a life that makes sense. Many have gotten far away from this truth- that God exists and that He wants us to know Him. He wants us to know He loves us right where we are and that He loves us too much to leave us there. He is here to heal us of the things that bind us up. He wants us to know Him in a personal way, which means He is a part of our whole life – not just a part we give Him on Sunday or a

Holiday. We have never needed to hear this message at any-time more than now. The Virgin Mary continuously asks for us to "Pray, Pray, Pray"! We are told in her messages from Medjugorje that we can change the course of events in our lives and the world through our prayers. She also tells us that we must spend time in prayer to truly know God. We believe that this relationship with Jesus begins with a prayerful plea from a heart that wants to know Him. This is where it began for us and this is where it can begin for you too. We are here to tell you, along with Mary, that God does exists and He cares for you deeply.

"Dear children! Also today I am with you and I am looking at you and blessing you, and I am not losing hope that this world will change for the good and that peace will reign in the hearts of men. Joy will begin to reign in the world because you have opened yourselves to my call and to God's love. The Holy Spirit is changing a multitude of those who have said 'yes'. Therefore I desire to say to you: thank you for having responded to my call."

Mary's Message of January 25, 2011

For this reason I knell before the Father, from whom his whole family in heaven and on earth derives its name. I pray that out of His glorious riches He may strengthen you with power though His Spirit in your inner being, so that Christ may dwell in your hearts through faith. And I pray that you, being rooted and established in love, may have power, together with all the Lord's holy people, to grasp how wide and long and high and deep is the love of Christ, and to know this love that surpasses knowledge - that you may be filled to the measure of all the fullness of God. Now to Him who is able to do immeasurably more that all we ask or imagine, according to His power that is at work within us, to Him be glory in the church (the body of believers) and in Christ Jesus throughout all generations, forever and ever! Amen.

Ephesians 3: 14-21
New International Version

Epilogue

Bob Schuchts

You have just read a very personal story about some amazing events that happened to Don and Judy in 1990. What speaks to me most in Don and Judy's story is that they came in without a close relationship with Christ at the time or any background in Catholicism. Much of what they experienced was strange and new to them- so I could trust that this was not coming from a personal religious belief system or from some kind of wishful thinking on their part.

This is one of the reasons why Don and Judy's story has had a significant impact in my own faith life. Let me explain: I had been hearing about the events and miracles in Medjugorje for several years before I met Judy and Don. I had heard of Mary's appearances to the children, I had heard of rosary's turning gold, of the miracles of the sun, of the number of lives that had reportedly been changed, and of the spiritual battle for those who tried to go. But I had been hearing all of it from Catholics, from those who went in with a Catholic belief system. In fact I knew many of the people with whom Don and Judy traveled to Medjugorje. I never met Terri, but I knew the Kearneys and Shovlains and several others who had been to Medjugorje on earlier pilgrimages. I knew each of these to be people of genuine faith. Their stories were credible. I tended to believe they were telling the truth. Though I believed these things really did happen, it never really affected me personally. That all changed for me with Don and Judy's trip.

Over the years, I have had time to reflect on why Don and Judy's experience impacted me so much. I realize one reason is that I saw all of this up close and heard it told so intimately. I saw the changes in Don and Judy happen before my own eyes. I knew them. I saw and heard their despair before these events. Then I saw and heard something completely different after these events. In Judy, I saw her joy and hope after she and Terri spoke. I saw Don's turmoil as he fought like crazy to avoid going (without him fully knowing why at the time), and his peace when he came back. In fact, I saw incredible changes in both of them when they returned. Jesus said you could test a true prophet by the fruits. When Judy came back from meeting with Terri- she was at peace, filled with joy, believed in God again, and was renewed in purpose and hope- in short everything changed for her. Then, when I saw Don after his trip to Medjugorje, it was even more remarkable. He went from being hard-hearted, proud, critical, and complaining (not all the time of course- but this was predominant) to a person who radiated Christ. He was humble, meek, full of love, tender-hearted, forgiving, accepting of himself, honest, and full of zeal. A man, who had never mentioned Jesus before, was now on fire in love with him. Make no mistake this was a real conversion- kind of like St. Paul's on the road to Damascus.

Their transformation was so great, that I believed they did not need my therapy services any more after they returned from Medjugorje and we decided not to reschedule. As it turns out, we were all a little naïve and overzealous. Even St. Paul struggled in the years following his conversion experience. So have Don and Judy. Our paths have crossed at key times over these past twenty-one years. They had moved away from Tallahassee and then came back a couple of years ago.

In those twenty-one years, I know they have faced many challenges. But through all of it they remain indelibly changed for the good. They have always remembered they had a refuge in the Lord. Testing the fruit twenty-one years later they both have a deep love for Him and to this day they still get emotional when they share their story. In short- what they experienced was real and from the Holy Spirit.

Don and Judy's radical conversion had a profound impact on me. Though they didn't know it at the time, their experience was an answer to some of my most earnest prayers.

In order for you to understand, I need to tell you a little more of my history. I grew up Catholic. I went to twelve years of Catholic school. I saw a mixture of genuine faith and external religious practices growing up in my family, at school, and at church. Mostly, our faith in God was important; mostly it was also genuine. But some of it, for me at least, didn't connect to my heart. All that was strange for Don and Judy (Priests, Eucharist, Adoration, Confession, Rosary, Devotion to Mary, etc.) was familiar to me. But not all of it was positive- some was positive, some neutral, and some had a negative connotation for me. I resonated with Jesus warning against "vain repetition" in prayer. To me the Mass, the rosary, and other devotions to Mary fell under the category of "vain repetitions", at least at times.

When I was fourteen years old, my parents divorced and my family moved to Florida. During the years following, my mother brought us to both Catholic and Protestant churches. To this day, some of my brothers and sisters are non-Catholic. I was equally influenced by Catholic and Protestant worship and teaching for many years. As a young adult, I would often go to both the Catholic Church and then also to a Baptist, Presbyterian, Episcopalian, Methodist, or Charismatic church with friends and family members. I naively dismissed all that was in conflict between the different factions of the Church as "man made". This meant all the distinctively Catholic aspects were relegated as unimportant or "disruptive of unity" in my mind. Of those "Catholic" beliefs and practices, ones concerning Mary and things like praying the rosary seemed to me the most divisive. I didn't believe I needed a priest to confess my sins to God; I didn't like the "rules" that kept non-Catholics from receiving Communion, etc. In short, I had become more Protestant in my thinking than Catholic in many ways.

When I heard about Medjugorje, I was confused. I saw the genuineness of the people sharing their stories, but I was not convinced. I remained neutral, perhaps slightly positive, but certainly not convicted enough to change my faith practices, by submitting to the messages of Medjugorje. In all I felt like it was too "Mary" focused. I could understand why Catholics were accused of being "Mary worshippers" by non-Catholics. I have never witnessed a Catholic worship Mary or put her in the place of God, but I did see what seemed to be an over emphasis on Mary and not enough on Jesus, the Father, and the Holy Spirit. (At the time, I didn't give much heed or know enough about the millions of lives that had been converted to Jesus Christ through Marian Apparitions throughout the world over the millennia.)

Everything began to change for me on the retreat where I had that encounter with the Holy Spirit. After that event, I was much more open and more dedicated to prayer. I fell in love with Jesus. I was given the grace to believe in Jesus' Real Presence in the Eucharist. I saw the need for confession with a priest, and practiced going to confession more often. So much that had been dead ritual, like the celebration of Mass, became deeply meaningful and spiritually moving for me. In short it was somewhat akin to going from black-and-white to color television. Everything was more alive, because my heart was more alive. I was more open to believe in miracles and in the supernatural realm than ever before.

I don't know when it began, but I remember praying earnestly to be able to know what to believe about Mary's role and how to consider practices like praying the rosary. How could I have a devotion to Mary that brought me closer to Jesus, more yielded to the Holy Spirit, more dependent on God my loving Father. These are the questions that plagued me before my encounters with Judy and Don. These were my earnest prayers before I met them, so you can see why their experiences became an answer to my own private prayers.

God's Providence was amazing in the way it all played out. Mary is the one who called Judy and Don to Medjugorje, through Terri, but Jesus was the one who changed Don's life. It kind of reminded me of the story of the Wedding at Cana in the Gospel of John. Mary is the one who initiated Jesus' first miracle, but it was Jesus, himself, who performed the miracle of transformation.

When the nuns prayed for Don, they saw a vision of Jesus on the other shore. When Fr. Jozo prayed over Don, Don saw the crown of thorns and knew it was Jesus. Don's encounter was with Jesus. It was trustworthy and true, and both he and Judy knew it. And when they told me, I knew it too. And yet, those experiences with Jesus invited Don and Judy to a whole new world. They saw angels, they saw miracles, and they came to love and honor Mary. They came to a place of understanding that Mary did not pose a threat to Jesus as Lord or to their Protestant faith. Instead, Mary always exalts Jesus and points the way to her Son.

So now you know how Don and Judy's encounter was an answer to my own prayers. Over the years, in large part influenced by Don and Judy's encounter, I too have come to see that Mary is not an obstacle to Jesus, but a bridge to Him. I now pray the rosary daily. I celebrate my Catholic faith more fully, understanding so much more than I ever did before, and recognizing there is so much more to learn. I love every part of my Catholic faith. And still, my passion for Christian unity has not lessened. It has grown even stronger. Don and Judy's experience gave me hope that the things that currently divide us, are in God's hands. Jesus himself prayed for Christian unity, and only the Holy Spirit will bring it. I am no longer ashamed of Mary, nor do I see her as a barrier to Christian unity. Rather, she is the mother of all Christians. As St. Augustine said, the Mother of the Head (Christ) is also Mother of the entire body. (See John 19:26-27; Revelation 12:17). Mary does not diminish Jesus role in salvation; she exalts Him, and sees herself as God's handmaiden. (see Luke 2) I can honestly say that I have come to love Mary. Rather than pull me away from Jesus, my relationship with her has only increased my love for and faith in Jesus. I first learned this in my heart from Judy and Don. Who would have guessed that it would take two fallen-away Baptists to teach this ambivalent Catholic to love his Mother Mary! And for all of us to become even more passionately in love with Jesus Christ.